SHAMBHALA DRAGON EDITIONS

The dragon is an age-old symbol of the highest spiritual essence, embodying wisdom, strength, and the divine power of transformation. In this spirit, Shambhala Dragon Editions offers a treasury of readings in the sacred knowledge of Asia. In presenting the works of authors both ancient and modern, we seek to make these teachings accessible to lovers of wisdom everywhere.

THE EXPERIENCE OF INSIGHT

A Simple and Direct Guide to Buddhist Meditation

Joseph Goldstein

Introduction by Ram Dass
Preface by Robert Hall

SHAMBHALA
BOSTON & LONDON
1987

Shambhala Publications, Inc.
Horticultural Hall
300 Massachusetts Avenue
Boston, Massachusetts 02115
http://www.shambhala.com

Printed in the United States of America
⊗ This edition is printed on acid-free paper that meets the
American National Standards Institute Z39.48 Standard.
Distributed in the United States by Random House, Inc.,
and in Canada by Random House of Canada Ltd

*The Library of Congress catalogs the original paperback
edition of this work as follows:*

Goldstein, Joseph, 1944–
    The experience of insight.
    Originally published: Santa Cruz, CA: Unity Press,
© 1976.
    Includes bibliographical references.
    1. Meditation (Buddhism).   I. Title.
BQ5612.G64   1983   294.3'443   82-42682
ISBN 0-87773-226-4 (pbk.)
ISBN 0-394-71430-X (Random House: pbk.)

Preface

Every so often, a book appears that has special value for people who are students of what is. I think of books like Suzuki Roshi's *Zen Mind, Beginner's Mind* and Carlos Castaneda's writings on the teachings of Don Juan. Here is another one.

This is the work of a teacher of meditation who is young, an American and, yet, who speaks from that empty, peaceful space usually associated with the old and wise ones from other cultures.

Joseph Goldstein is a unique teacher. Like all good teachers, he is a vehicle for re-introducing the ancient knowledge into the confusion of this modern world. His words ring clearly, because they are born from his own experience. He has spent many years studying and practicing the life of meditation while living in India. Now he is bringing to this country a depth of understanding that could only come from those years of practice.

He teaches meditation as a method of learning to see things as they are. His discourses are practical instructions for learning how to live with detachment and compassion. And throughout his work, he keeps that one quality essential for being a truly human teacher—a sense of humor.

This is a good book. It is a portrait of Joseph at work, but it also presents an actual record of the dynamics of a course in meditation. Courses, such as the one described here, guided by Joseph and his co-workers, are intense experiences in the practice of Insight Meditation. They are conducted in silence, except for the discourses and question/answer periods. The daily schedule of sitting and walking practice begins each day at 5:00 AM and extends into the late evenings, and even longer for the serious students. There are usually from 50 to 200 students practicing together, sharing a process that may include visits to hell, rides into bliss, and any other experience the mind can possibly provide.

For myself, a psychiatrist working outside the orthodox theories of my profession, Joseph has been a welcome inspiration and a wonderful friend. His understanding of the mind springs from direct confrontation, rather than the study of intellectual concepts. What he teaches is relevant and useful for all of us concerned with freedom—the liberation that only comes from the light of insight.

I hope that many of my colleagues in the helping professions find this book in their hands. It could introduce a refreshing new perspective for their work, just as knowing Joseph and the people who work with him has done for me.

Robert K. Hall, M.D.
Lomi School
San Francisco
December, 1975

Introduction

During my studies in India, one of the teachers who most perfectly embodied his teaching was Anagarika Munindra. The ephemeral nature of phenomena, including self, was no better demonstrated than in his absent presence. Originally a Krishnabhakta with Ananda Mayi Ma, he was drawn to Burma to pursue a Theravadin Buddhist *sadhana*. For many years Munindra so successfully absorbed the Pali Canon of Buddhism, an exact and complex no-nonsense blueprint of the mind, and the manner in which illusion is created and dispelled, that when I met him in Bodhgaya I found it difficult to differentiate him from the doctrine.

Despite the fact that Munindra-ji held a number of responsible administrative positions in the sacred city where Buddha had attained enlightenment, he commenced teaching. Among the students of this physically diminutive teacher was Joseph, a very tall young westerner who impressed me immediately by his power, simplicity and quiet dignity. Like me, Joseph retained his western acculturation and yet was drinking deeply from the well of another culture's insight into liberation, fully aware of the universality of the spirit.

After many years of patient study, Joseph returned to his homeland and quite humbly and simply began to offer ten day to three month long, inexpensive meditation retreats throughout the U.S. Because of my deep respect for him I was truly delighted that the west was to be blessed by his teaching. I sensed in him what I had sensed in his teacher—a being who could be identified with his teaching.

The living transmission of a formal teaching is a delicate matter. In the lectures transcribed in this volume we have a good example. For Joseph is another of those beings who could be called (as Jung referred to Richard Wilhelm) a 'gnostic intermediary'; that is, one who transmits a teaching from one culture and age to another not via his intellect but through absorption into his blood and gut so that he, in truth, becomes the teaching.

Such an incorporation, a 'grokking,' a marital union, an identity, requires that 'surrender' to which spiritual teachings refer again and again. Such a person who is a living transmission of any teaching is the statement of the faith and surrender necessary to receive the true meaning of the work; i.e., that to which the word refers.

It is now apparent, following so much cynicism in the late 50's and early 60's, that our multifaceted exploration of the later 60's has matured into a deep and genuine spiritual seeking by literally hundreds of thousands of beings who have taken birth in the western hemisphere. I understand these past years to be a process of tuning to the *dharma* in a way which has retained integrity with our evolving consciousness.

Now many of us seek the deeper, purer, more esoteric teachings. And we recognize that in order to receive these teachings we must assume a meditative stance. Thus, there is an increasing demand for meditation training as both means and end. The meditation course from which the transcripts in this volume have been drawn is a highly significant contribution to our growth at this time.

This book is a blessing to which I add my own.

Ram Dass
Lama, New Mexico
July 1975

Acknowledgments

So many thanks to

STEPHEN LEVINE, Dharma friend and editor, who has untiringly nursed this project to completion.

SHARON SALZBERG, invaluable colleague in teaching and mainstay of loving support, who contributed greatly both to several chapters of this book and to its general editing.

JACK KORNFELD, co-teacher and unfailing inspiration in the Dharma.

RICHARD BARSKY, friend and associate in teaching.

SUSAN OLSHUFF, CATHY INGRAM, LIZA JONES and DONNA SPIETH who so beautifully offered their services for the monumental task of transcribing tapes and typing manuscripts.

RICHARD COHEN and CHAITANYA for their wit and skill in editing and

ROBERT HALL and RAM DASS for their kind introductions and their encouragement throughout which gave strength to this entire undertaking.

Grateful acknowledgment is made to the following for permission to use their fine materials:

Rene Daumal, MOUNT ANALOGUE, translated by Roger Shattuck. Copyright 1959 by Vincent Stuart Limited. Reprinted by permission of Pantheon Books, a division of Random House, Inc.

Hermann Hesse, SIDDHARTHA, translated by Holda Rosner. Copyright 1951 by New Directions Publishing Corporation. Reprinted by permission of New Directions Publishing Corporation.

Thomas Merton, THE WAY OF CHUANG TZU. Copyright 1965 by the Abbey of Gethsemani. Reprinted by permission of New Directions Publishing Corporation.

Hui Neng, PLATFORM SUTRA, translated by A. F. Price and Wong Mou-Lam. Reprinted by permission of Shambhala Publications.

Nyanatiloka, PATH TO DELIVERANCE. Reprinted by permission of The Buddha Sahitya Sabha, Colombo and the Buddhist Publication Society, Kandy, Ceylon.

Suzuki Roshi, ZEN MIND, BEGINNER'S MIND. Copyright 1970 John Weatherhill Inc. Reprinted by permission of John Weatherhill Incorporated.

Han Shan, COLD MOUNTAIN, translated by Burton Watson. Copyright 1970 by Columbia University Press. Reprinted by permission of Columbia University Press.

Chuang Tsu, INNER CHAPTERS, translated by Gia-fu Feng and Jane English. Copyright 1974 by Gia-fu Feng and Jane English. Reprinted by permission of Alfred A. Knopf, Inc.

Wei Wu Wei, POSTHUMOUS PIECES, copyright 1968 by Wei Wu Wei. Reprinted by permission of Hong Kong University Press.

Table of Contents

To my teachers, with the greatest love and respect

Anagarika Sri Munindra
Sri S. N. Goenka
Mrs. Nani Bala Barua

and to my mother, Evelyn, whose acceptance and support was an inestimable aid on the journey.

•

Opening and Beginning Instruction

A traditional beginning for meditation retreats is taking refuge in the Buddha, Dharma and Sangha. To take refuge in the Buddha means acknowledging the seed of enlightenment that is within ourselves, the possibility of freedom. It also means taking refuge in those qualities which the Buddha embodies, qualities like fearlessness, wisdom, love and compassion. Taking refuge in the Dharma means taking refuge in the law, in the way things are; it is acknowledging our surrender to the truth, allowing the Dharma to unfold within us. Taking refuge in the Sangha means taking support in the community, in all of us helping one another towards enlightenment and freedom.

An indispensable foundation for meditation practice is following certain moral precepts. It is a way of maintaining a basic purity of body, speech, and mind. The five precepts which should be followed are: not killing, which means refraining from knowingly taking any life, not even swatting a mosquito or stepping on an ant; not stealing, which means not taking anything which is not given; refraining from sexual misconduct, which in the context of this retreat means observing celibacy; not lying or speaking falsely or harshly; and not taking intoxicants, which again in the context of the meditation course means not taking alcohol or drugs. Following these precepts will provide a strong base for the development of concentration, and will make the growth of insight possible.

We are all sharing something very special in having the opportunity to be here, to look within ourselves in this quiet and secluded setting. It is rare to have an entire month devoted to meditation, to finding out about ourselves, about who we are. There are a few attitudes which will be helpful in maintaining a serious and balanced effort. The first of these is patience: there are times when the month will seem endless and everyone will be wondering, particularly at four-thirty on cold mornings, exactly what they are doing here. In the course of the meditation practice there will be many ups and downs. There will be times when the meditation is good and beautiful and insightful, and times when it will be boring, painful, full of restlessness and doubt. Being patient throughout all these experiences will help to keep the mind in balance. Someone once asked Trungpa Rinpoche where "grace" fit into the Buddhist tradition. He replied that grace is patience. If we have a patient mind, all things will unfold in a natural and organic way. Patience means staying in a state of balance regardless of what is happening, staying easy and relaxed and alert.

Milarepa, the famous Tibetan yogi, advised his disciples to "hasten slowly." Hasten in the sense of being continuous and unrelenting in your effort, but do so with poise and equanimity. Persistent and full of effort, yet very relaxed and balanced.

Another aid for deepening meditation is silence. We don't often get a good look at what's happening in our minds because talking distracts our attention and dissipates our energy. Much of the energy that is conserved by not talking can be used for the development of awareness and mindfulness. As with the meditation practice itself, silence too should be easy and relaxed. This does not mean talking when you want to, but just relaxing into the silence, going through the day quietly aware. By keeping silence, the whole range of mental and physical activity will become extremely clear; verbal silence makes possible a deeper silence of mind.

Interaction between friends or couples is discouraged. Try to cultivate a sense of aloneness. To do this, it is helpful to suspend preconceptions about yourselves, about relationships, about other people. Take this time to experience yourself deeply.

We are each going to die alone. It is necessary to come to terms with our basic aloneness, to become comfortable with it. The mind can become strong and peaceful in that understanding, making possible a beautiful communion with others. When we understand ourselves, then relationships become easy and meaningful.

It is also helpful not to mix different practices. Many of you have done various kinds of meditation. For this period of time it would be good to concentrate solely on the development of Vipassana, or insight. It is through the cultivation of mindfulness that insight develops. Concentrating all efforts during this month on the development of moment to moment mindfulness will prevent superficiality of practice. If all efforts are directed towards one goal, the mind will become powerful and penetrating.

There is also great value in slowing down. There is no hurry, no place to go, nothing else to do, just a settling back into the moment. In all activities during the day be very mindful, notice carefully all your movements. The meditation deepens through the continuity of awareness.

We'll begin the sitting practice with a very simple object of awareness: mindfulness of breathing. Assume any posture that is comfortable to you, keeping the back reasonably straight, without being stiff or strained. If you are in a cramped or bent-over position, you will more quickly become uncomfortable. You can sit in a chair if you like. The important thing is not to move very often. The eyes should be closed, unless you have been trained in a technique where they are kept slightly open, and you prefer to do that. Keeping the eyes open is merely a way of putting them someplace and then forgetting about them. Generally it seems easier if they're closed in a relaxed way. But it doesn't matter.

Awareness of the breath can be practiced in one of two ways. When you breathe in, the abdomen naturally rises or extends and when you breathe out, it falls. Keep your attention on the movement of the abdomen, not imagining, not visualizing anything, just experiencing the sensation of the movement. Don't control or force the breath in any way, merely stay attentive to the rising, falling movement of the abdomen.

The alternative is to be aware of the breath as it goes in and out of the nostrils, keeping the attention in the area around the tip of the nose or upper lip. Maintain the attention on the breath much as a watchman standing at a gate observes people passing in and out. Don't follow the breath all the way down or all the way out; don't control or force the breathing. Simply be aware of the in and out breath as it passes the nostrils. It is helpful in the beginning of practice to make mental notes either of "rising, falling" or "in, out." This aids in keeping the mind on the object.

In the first few minutes see which object appears more clearly, either the rising, falling or the in, out. Then choose one place of attention and stay with it, do not go back and forth. If at times it becomes less distinct, don't switch to the other object thinking it's going to be easier. Once you have decided where you're going to cultivate your attention keep it there and try to remain with it through all the changes. It is sometimes clear, sometimes not, sometimes deep, sometimes shallow, sometimes long, sometimes short. Remember, it is not a breathing exercise; it is the beginning exercise in mindfulness.

The walking meditation is done by noticing the lifting, forward and placing movement of the foot in each step. It is helpful to finish one step completely before lifting the other foot. "Lifting, moving, placing, lifting, moving, placing." It is very simple. Again it is not an exercise in movement. It is an exercise in mindfulness. Use the movement to develop a careful awareness. In the course of the day, you can expect many changes. Sometimes you may feel like walking more quickly, sometimes very slowly. You can take the steps as a single unit, "stepping, stepping." Or you may start out walking quickly and, in that same walking meditation, slow down until you are dividing it again into the three parts. Experiment. The essential thing is to be mindful, to be aware of what's happening.

In walking, the hands should remain stationary either behind the back, at the sides, or in front. It's better to look a little ahead, and not at your feet, in order to avoid being involved in the concept of "foot" arising from the visual contact. All of the attention should be on experiencing the movement, feeling the sensations of the lifting, forward, placing motions.

This is the schedule to give you an idea of how the days will progress.

4:30	— awakening
5:00–6:30	— walk and sit
6:30–7:30	— breakfast
7:30–8:00	— walking
8:00–9:00	— group sitting
9:00–9:45	— walking
9:45–10:45	— group sitting
10:45–11:30	— walking
11:30–1:15	— lunch and rest
1:15–2:00	— group sitting
2:00–2:45	— walking
2:45–3:45	— group sitting
3:45–5:00	— walk and sit
5:00–5:30	— tea
5:30–6:00	— walking
6:00–7:00	— group sitting

7:00–8:00   — talk
8:00–8:45   — walking
8:45–9:45   — group sitting
9:45–10:00   — tea
10:00–   — further practice or sleep

The schedule will be posted. For the first few days or week, try to follow it as much as possible. As you become comfortable spending the day meditatively, in a continuous effort of mindfulness, you will discover your own pace. Just sit and walk as continuously as possible. Take meals, as all activities, with mindfulness and awareness. After some time you might like to walk longer, to walk for an hour or an hour and a half, and then sit. Some people like to sit longer, for two or three hours at a time; perhaps some of you will like to stay up late at night. When I was first practicing in India, I meditated in the very late night hours: the time between midnight and three I found peaceful and quiet and good for practice. As the meditation gets stronger, less and less sleep is needed. Go to sleep when you feel really tired, not just out of habit at a certain hour. It may be that as the meditation develops, you will not feel tired at all and can keep up the practice day and night. Try to feel out what is comfortable for you, what maximizes the effort without forcing or straining.

Saint Francis de Sales wrote,

Be patient with everyone, but above all, with yourself. I mean, do not be disheartened by your imperfections, but always rise up with fresh courage. I am glad you make a fresh beginning daily. There is no better means of attainment to the spiritual life than by continually beginning again, and never thinking that we have done enough. How are we to be patient in dealing with our neighbor's faults if we are impatient in dealing with our own. He who is fretted by his own failings will not correct them. All profitable correction comes from a calm and peaceful mind.

•

Noble Eightfold Path

We have all begun a journey. A journey into our minds. A journey of discovery and exploration of who and what we are. Taking the first step is difficult, and in the first days of practice there is often restlessness, or sleepiness, some boredom, laziness, doubt, and perhaps regret about getting involved at all. The first step is difficult for everyone. Spinoza, at the end of one of his important philosophical works, wrote, "All noble things are as difficult as they are rare." The spiritual quest we are embarking upon is a rare and precious undertaking, so be gentle yet persevering through any beginning difficulties.

A beautiful allegory for this journey is the book *Mount Analogue.* The story is of a group of people searching for a mountain. The base of the mountain is on the earth while the summit represents the highest possible spiritual attainment. Initially, the pilgrims are faced with a great obstacle: under ordinary circumstances the mountain is invisible, and considerable struggle and hardship is undergone just to locate it. After much effort, they find the mountain and are able to approach its base. The rest of the book describes all the preparations, difficulties, struggles and excitement of beginning the ascent to the top.

We're on this very same journey, ascending the mountain of spiritual insight. We have already discovered the secret of its invisibility: the fact that the truth, the law, the Dharma, is within us, not outside of ourselves, and that we begin from where we are.

The path up the mountain, the path to freedom, has been well-mapped by the many people who have walked upon it. One of the clearest of these descriptions is found in the teachings of the Buddha, expressed as the noble eightfold path. It is a map, and a guide pointing the way to enlightenment.

The first step of this path up the mountain is right understanding. It is, in fact, both the first step and the last. It is because of some degree of understanding we begin the journey in the first place; and that understanding is brought to completion, to perfection, at the summit when we penetrate to the very deepest levels of our mind. In the beginning, right understanding deals with certain natural laws which govern our everyday lives. One of the most important of these is the law of karma, the law of cause and effect. Every action brings a certain result. Things are not happening to us by chance or accident. Whenever we act motivated by greed, hatred or delusion, pain and suffering come back to us. When our actions are motivated by generosity, love or wisdom, the results are happiness and peace. If we integrate this understanding of the law of karma into our lives, we can begin more consciously to cultivate and develop wholesome states of mind.

The Buddha often stressed the power and importance of generosity. Giving is the expression in action of non-greed in the mind. The whole spiritual path involves letting go, not grasping, not clinging, and generosity is the manifestation of that non-attachment.

Another part of right understanding is acknowledging the special relationship, the unique karma, we have with our parents, and the responsibilities and obligations we have to them. Our parents cared for us when we were unable to care for ourselves, and it is due to their concern at a time when we were helpless that we now have the opportunity to practice the Dharma. The Buddha said that there is no way of repaying this debt, that we could carry our parents about on our shoulders for an entire lifetime and still we would not have fulfilled our obligation. The only way of repaying our parents is to help establish them in the Dharma, in the truth, in right understanding. Generally, we spend a great deal of time and energy freeing ourselves psychologically from our parents, which certainly has its value, but in that space of freedom, we should recognize our responsibility towards them.

Right understanding also involves a profound and subtle knowledge of our true nature. In the course of meditation practice it becomes increasingly clear that everything is impermanent. All the elements of mind and body exist in a moment and pass away, arising and vanishing continuously. The breath comes in and goes out, thoughts arise and pass away, sensations come into being and vanish. All phenomena are in constant flux. There is no lasting security to be had in this flow of impermanence. And deep insight into the selfless nature of all elements begins to offer a radically different perspective on our lives and the world. The mind stops grasping and clinging when the microscopic transience of everything is realized, and when we experience the process of mind and body without the burden of self. This is the kind of right understanding that is developed in meditation through careful and penetrating observation.

The second step of the eightfold path is right thought. This means thoughts free of sense desire, free of ill will, free of cruelty. As long as the mind is attached to sense desire, it will seek after external objects, external fulfillments which, because of their impermanent nature, cannot be finally satisfying. There is a momentary experience of pleasure and then craving returns for more. The endless cycle of desire for sense pleasures keeps the mind in turbulence and confusion. Freeing thought from sense desires does not mean suppressing them and pretending they are not there. If a desire is suppressed, it will usually manifest in some other way. Equally unskillful is identifying with each desire as it arises and compulsively acting on it. Right thought means becoming aware of sense desires and letting them go. The more we let go, the lighter the mind becomes. Then there is no disturbance, no tension, and we begin to free ourselves from our storehouse of conditioning, from our bondage to sense desires.

Freedom from ill will means freedom from anger. Anger is a burning in the mind, and when expressed causes great suffering to others as well. It is helpful to be able to recognize anger and to let it go. Then the mind becomes light and easy, expressing its natural lovingkindness.

Thoughts free of cruelty mean thoughts of compassion, feeling for the suffering of others and wanting to alleviate it. We should develop thoughts which are completely free of cruelty towards any living thing.

The next steps on the path up the mountain have to do with how we relate in the world; how we relate to our environment, to other people. They are a prescription for putting us into harmony with our surroundings, for establishing a proper ecology of mind so that we're not in discord with others or with nature around us. The first aspect of relating to the world in this way is right speech. Right speech means not speaking what is untrue, or using slanderous, abusive or harsh language; rather, speaking words which are honest and helpful, creating a vibration of peace and harmony.

There is a story told of the Buddha returning after his enlightenment to the city where his family was still living. Many relatives and friends, inspired by his presence, by his love and compassion and wisdom, joined the order of monks. At that time, Rahula, his son, also became a novice in the order. There is one famous discourse called *Advice to Rahula* in which the Buddha, speaking to his son, said that under no circumstances, either for his own benefit or for the benefit of others, should he speak that which is untrue. So important is the commitment to truth. It makes our relationships easy and uncomplicated. Honesty in speech also reflects back to honesty with ourselves. There are many things in our mind and body, tensions of all kinds, unpleasantness, things we don't like to look at, things about which we're untruthful with ourselves. Truthfulness in speech becomes the basis for being honest in our own minds, and that is when things begin to open up. We then begin to see clearly, working through all the neuroses of mind.

The fourth step of the path up the mountain is right action. This means not killing, minimizing the amount of pain we inflict on other beings; not stealing, that is, not taking what isn't given; and not committing sexual misconduct, which in the context of our daily life can be most basically understood as not causing suffering to others out of greed or desire for pleasant sensations.

Often, we are unaware in the moment of the long range effects of our actions. There is a story from *Mount Analogue* which illustrates this.

There was a rule for people who were climbing the mountain that above a certain point no living things were to be killed. The climbers had to carry all their food. One day someone who was walking on the mountain above that point was caught in a violent snowstorm. For three days he lived in a makeshift shelter with no food in near freezing conditions. On the third day the blizzard ended. He saw a very old rat crawling out of a hole and thought there would be no harm in killing the rat so that he could feed himself and get down the mountain. Somehow he managed to get a stone and kill the rat. He made it down the mountain and did not think any more about it. Some time later he was called before the tribunal of guides, people responsible for the mountain and the path. He was called to account for the killing of the rat, an event which by this time he had forgotten. It seems there had been serious consequences. The rat, being very old, was not strong enough to catch the healthy insects, and fed on the diseased insect population. So when the rat was killed there was no natural check on the diseased insects. Disease spread throughout the whole species and they died off. The insects had been responsible for pollinating and fertilizing much of the plant growth on the mountainside. When the insects died off, without this fertilization the vegetation started to diminish. The plant life had been holding the soil in place and when the vegetation began to die the soil started to erode. Eventually, there was a great landslide which killed many people who were climbing up the mountain, and blocked the path for a long time. All of this the outcome of the seemingly insignificant act of killing the old rat.

Because we're not always able to see the far-reaching consequences of each of our acts, we should take care not to create disturbances in the environment but to emanate peacefulness and gentleness, love and compassion.

The next step of the eightfold path involving our relationships in the world is right livelihood. This means doing that kind of work for support and maintenance which is not harmful to others; not having work which involves killing, stealing or dishonesty. There is a traditional list of occupations which are unskillful, such as dealing in weapons or intoxicants, hunting or fishing, all causing suffering to others. The Dharma is not just sitting. Sitting is a powerful tool for understanding, but wisdom and understanding have to be integrated into our lives. Right livelihood is an important part of the integration: "To walk in a sacred manner as was the American Indian way. To make an art of life." To do what we do in a sacred manner. To do what we do with awareness.

The next three steps on the path have to do primarily with the practice of meditation. The first of these is in many respects the most important: right effort. Unless we make the effort, nothing happens. It is said in the Abhidharma, the Buddhist psychology, that effort is the root of all achievement, the foundation of all attainment. If we want to get to the top of the mountain and just sit at the bottom thinking about it, it's not going to happen. It is through the effort, the actual climbing of the mountain, the taking of one step after another, that the summit is reached. Ramana Maharshi, a great sage of modern India, wrote, "No one succeeds without effort. Mind control is not your birthright. Those who succeed owe their success to their perseverance." But effort has to be balanced. Being very tense and anxious is a great hindrance. Energy has to be balanced with tranquility. It is as if you are trying to tune the strings on a guitar. If they are too tight or too loose, the sound is not right. In our practice also, we have to be persistent and persevering but with a relaxed and balanced mind, making the effort without forcing. There is so much to discover in ourselves, so many levels of mind to understand. By making effort, the path unfolds. No one is going to do it for us. No one can enlighten another being. The Buddha's enlightenment solved his problem, it didn't solve ours . . . except to point out the way. We each have to walk the path for ourselves.

Mindfulness is the seventh step in this noble eightfold path, and it means being aware of what is happening in the present moment. It means noticing the flow of things: when walking, to be aware of the movement of the body; in observing the breath, to be aware of the sensations of the in-out or rising-falling; to notice thoughts or feelings as they arise. As expressed by one Zen master, "When you walk, walk; when you run, run; above all, don't wobble." Whatever the object is, to notice it, to be aware of it, without grasping, which is greed, without condemning, which is hatred, without forgetting, which is delusion; just observing the flow, observing the process. When mindfulness is cultivated it becomes very rhythmic and the whole day becomes a dance. Mindfulness brings the qualities of poise, equilibrium and balance to the mind, keeping it sharply focused, with the attitude of sitting back and watching the passing show.

The last step on the path up the mountain is right concentration. This is one-pointedness of mind, the ability of the mind to stay steady on an object. The first days of this journey may seem difficult because concentration is not yet well developed. To climb a mountain, you need a certain physical strength. If you are not yet very strong, in the beginning you will feel tired and uncomfortable. But as the body gets stronger, climbing becomes easier. It is the same in meditation. As concentration is developed, it becomes less difficult to stay in the moment. The hindrances that are faced in the beginning of practice are then easily overcome.

If you put a kettle on the stove and every few minutes take the lid off, it will take a longer time for the water to boil. If you put the kettle on the stove and leave it there, the water will heat up very quickly.

A meditation retreat is a unique opportunity to develop a high degree of concentration and mindfulness. By being continuous in the practice, each moment builds on the one before, and in a short time the mind develops an acute strength and penetrating power.

The journey that we are on combines right relationship in the world with a deepening understanding and insight into our own nature. There is appropriate advice in *Mount Analogue* about ascending this path of wisdom: "Keep your eye fixed on the path to the top. But don't forget to look right in front of you. The last step depends upon the first. Don't think that you're there just because you see the summit. Watch your footing. Be sure of the next step. But don't let that distract you from the highest goal. The first step depends upon the last."

Being grounded in the present, cultivating awareness of the moment, and trusting our vision of freedom.

Question: *I notice that sensations seem stronger on the inbreath; this tends to upset my concentration. Is there anything I can do?*

Answer: The breath is a very interesting object of meditation because there's a great range of texture and intensity to it. Sometimes it's strong and heavy, sometimes it's fine and light. It can change between an inbreath and outbreath or it can change over a period of time. Sometimes the breath gets almost imperceptible. What makes the breath a valuable object of meditation is that when the breath becomes fine we can use it to draw the mind down to that level of subtlety. When you feel the breath getting more subtle, make the mind fine enough to stay aware of it. It takes an added energy—not of doing anything, but of silence.

How can you tell if a person is enlightened?

An enlightened being is untraceable. There is no possible way to perceive a free mind through any of the senses because it's beyond mind. It's like trying to locate a fire that has gone out. Where are you going to look for it? You can't think of enlightenment in terms of existing someplace. There is no special mark on the forehead; but you can recognize the qualities of wisdom and compassion in people, and honor those qualities.

About our relationship with our parents and the responsibility to try to show them the way. My parents wonder why I'm here and what I'm doing, but there seems no way to make them understand?

There are many ways of communicating—speech often not being the best. If you're with your parents, or any other people, and are very cooled out, non-judgmental, accepting, full of love and generosity, you don't have to say a word. Your own being at peace creates a certain space. It takes a long time. People are attached to their own way of looking at things. As soon as you say something that in any way threatens it, they become defensive. So the way is not to threaten, just to be the way you are, letting the Dharma unfold. A peaceful mind has its effect on its surroundings. It takes time and it takes patience, and a lot of love.

During the sitting meditation I found myself visualizing my breath as water flowing back and forth in a tunnel. Would it be more mindful to sit without the visualization?

Yes. The essence of the practice is to bring the mind to an experiential level rather than a conceptual one. Visualization of the breath is a concept. That's not what's happening; that's a projection onto it. The idea is to be with the experience of the sensations of the breath, not creating a concept around it.

How does devotion to God fit into the practice?

It depends upon what you mean by God. People have many different meanings for that word. One could equate God with the highest truth, which would be the same as the Dharma, the law, the way things are. The way of surrendering is letting go. Letting the Dharma unfold.

•

Instruction: Feelings

The mental factor of feeling is particularly important in the development of insight. Feeling refers to the quality of pleasantness, unpleasantness or neutrality which is present in every moment of consciousness. It is this quality of pleasantness or unpleasantness which has conditioned our mind to cling and condemn; grasping at pleasant objects and feelings, condemning and having aversion for unpleasant ones. When we become mindful of feelings we can begin to observe them with detachment and balance.

One class of objects in which feeling is predominant is physical sensations in the body. We can clearly experience sensations as being pleasant or painful. Being attentive to these sensations is a good way of developing mindfulness of feeling: experiencing bodily sensations without clinging to the blissful, light, tingling feelings, and without aversion to pain or tension. Simply observe all the sensations— heat, cold, itching, vibration, lightness, heaviness—and the associated feelings as they arise, without clinging or condemning or identifying with them.

Begin the sitting being aware of either the rising-falling of the abdomen or the in-out of the breath. Then as sensations become predominant in the body, give full attention, full mindfulness to them. It is important to keep a relaxed mind in observing the sensations, especially when there are strong painful feelings in the body. There is a tendency for the mind and body to tense in reaction to pain. This is an expression of aversion, dislike, avoidance, and creates an unbalanced state of mind; relax behind the pain and observe the flow. When the mind is silent, relaxed and attentive, pain is experienced not as a solid mass but as a flow, arising and vanishing moment to moment. Sit with a relaxed and calm mind, observing the flow of sensations, without aversion, without expectations.

Pain is a good object of meditation. When there's a strong pain in the body, the concentration becomes strong. The mind stays on it easily, without wandering very much. Whenever sensations in the body are predominant make them objects of meditation. When they are no longer predominant, return to the breath. The awareness should be rhythmic, not jumping or clutching at objects, just watching "rising-falling," "pain," "itching," "heat," "cold," "rising-falling." When you find yourself tensing because of pain, carefully examine the quality of unpleasantness, the quality of painfulness. Become mindful of that feeling and the mind will naturally come to a state of balance.

18

FOURTH
EVENING

•

Bare Attention

There is an ancient prophecy which says that twenty five hundred years after the Buddha's death a great revival and flourishing of the Dharma will take place. We are presently experiencing the truth of this in the renaissance of spiritual practice now happening. In order to have an appreciation of the breadth and scope of the prophecy it is helpful to understand what the word "Dharma" means. Dharma is a Sanskrit word and its most general meaning is the law, the way things are, the process of things, the Tao, and more specifically, the teachings of the Buddha: all of this is the Dharma. It also means each of the individual psychic and physical elements which comprise all beings. The elements of mind: thoughts, visions, emotions, consciousness, and the elements of matter, individually are called "dharmas." The task of all spirtual work is to explore and discover these dharmas within us, to uncover and penetrate all the elements of the mind and body, becoming aware of each of them individually, as well as understanding the laws governing their process and relationship. This is what we're doing here: experiencing in every moment the truth of our nature, the truth of who and what we are.

There is one quality of mind which is the basis and foundation of spiritual discovery, and that quality of mind is called "bare attention." Bare attention means observing things as they are, without choosing, without comparing, without evaluating, without laying our projections and expectations on to what is happening; cultivating instead a choiceless and non-interfering awareness.

This quality of bare attention is well expressed by a famous Japanese haiku:

> *The old pond.*
> *A frog jumps in.*
> *Plop!*

No dramatic description of the sunset and the peaceful evening sky over the pond and how beautiful it was. Just a crystal clear perception of what it was that happened. "The old pond; a frog jumps in; Plop!" Bare attention: learning to see and observe, with simplicity and directness. Nothing extraneous. It is a powerfully penetrating quality of mind.

As the quality of bare attention is developed it begins to effect certain basic changes in the way we live our lives. The watchwords of our time are "be here now"—living in the present moment. The problem is how to do it. Our minds are mostly dwelling in the past, thinking about things that have already happened, or planning for the future, imagining what is about to happen, often with anxiety or worry. Reminiscing about the past, fantasizing about the future; it is generally very difficult to stay grounded in the present moment. Bare attention is that quality of awareness which keeps us alive and awake in the here and now. Settling back into the moment, experiencing fully what it is that's happening.

There is a Zen story about living in the moment. Two monks were returning home in the evening to their temple. It had been raining and the road was very muddy. They came to an intersection where a beautiful girl was standing, unable to cross the street because of the mud. Just in the moment, the first monk picked her up in his arms and carried her across. The monks then continued on their way. Later that night the second monk, unable to restrain himself any longer, said to the first, "How could you do that?! We monks should not even look at females, much less touch them. Especially young and beautiful ones." "I left the girl there," the first monk said, "are you still carrying her?" As the quality of bare attention develops, noticing what's happening in and around us, we begin to experience and respond to the present with greater spontaneity and freedom.

Bare attention also brings the mind to a state of rest. An untrained mind is often reactive, clinging to what is pleasant and condemning what is unpleasant, grasping what is liked, pushing away what is disliked, reacting with greed and hatred. A tiring imbalance of mind. As bare attention is cultivated more and more we learn to experience our thoughts and feelings, situations and other people, without the tension of attachment or aversion. We begin to have a full and total experience of what it is that's happening, with a restful and balanced mind.

The awareness of bare attention is not limited to a certain time of sitting in the morning and evening. To think that sitting meditation is the time for awareness and the rest of the day is not, fragments our lives and undermines a real growth of understanding. Mindfulness is applicable and appropriate in each moment, whether we are sitting, standing, lying down, talking or eating. We should cultivate the state of bare attention on all objects, on all states of mind, in all situations. Every moment should be lived completely and wholeheartedly. There is a story of a man fleeing a tiger. He came to a precipice and catching hold of a wild vine, swung down over the edge. The tiger sniffed at him from above while below another tiger growled and snapped waiting for him to fall. As he hung there two mice began to gnaw away the vine. Just then he saw a big wild strawberry growing nearby. Reaching out with his free hand he plucked the strawberry. How sweet it tasted!

Another quality of bare attention is that when developed through a period of training it becomes effortless, it starts to work by itself. It's similar to the process one undergoes when learning to play a musical instrument. We sit down, take a few lessons, and are given certain exercises. We begin to practice, and at first the fingers don't move very easily; they hit a lot of wrong notes and it sounds terrible. But every day we practice, and gradually the fingers start to move more easily, the music starts to sound more beautiful. After a certain period of time, a proficiency develops so that the playing becomes effortless. At that time there is no difference between playing and practice; the playing itself is the practice. In just the same way, as we practice awareness, we start out very slowly, aware of the movement of each step, "lifting," "moving," "placing," aware of the breath, "rising, falling," or "in, out." In the beginning great effort is required. There are many gaps in the mindfulness. There are a lot of struggles and hindrances. But as the mind becomes trained in being aware, in being mindful, it becomes increasingly natural. There is a certain point in the practice when the momentum of mindfulness is so strong that it starts working by itself, and we begin to do things with an ease and simplicity and naturalness which is born out of this effortless awareness.

Bare attention is very much learning how to listen to our minds, our bodies, our environment. Perhaps at some time you have sat quietly by the side of an ocean or river. At first there is one big rush of sound. But in sitting quietly, doing nothing but listening, we begin to hear a multitude of fine and subtle sounds, the waves hitting against the shore, or the rushing current of the river. In that peacefulness and silence of mind we experience very deeply what is happening. It is just the same when we listen to ourselves; at first all we can hear is one "self" or "I." But slowly this self is revealed as a mass of changing elements, thoughts, feelings, emotions, and im-

ages, all illuminated simply by listening, by paying attention.
There's a beautiful poem by a Zen nun:

> *Sixty-six times have these eyes beheld the*
> *changing scenes of autumn.*
> *I have said enough about moonlight; ask me*
> *no more.*
> *Only listen to the voice of pines and cedars*
> *when no wind stirs.*

To hear the sounds of the trees when no wind stirs. The
peacefulness of that mind expresses the balance of the Tao, the
creative and receptive. It is creative in the sense of being alert,
penetrating and actively attentive. It is receptive in its choiceless-
ness, without discriminating or judging. It is a very open and soft
mind. When alertness and clarity of perception are combined with
receptivity and acceptance, the balance becomes complete, and the
mind experiences a perfect harmony of poise and equilibrium.

There are two mental factors which are primarily responsible for
the development of bare attention. The first is concentration, the
ability of the mind to stay steady on an object. The other factor is
mindfulness, which notices what is happening in the moment, not
allowing the mind to become forgetful; it keeps the mind grounded
and collected. When mindfulness and concentration are both developed, a balance of mind is achieved, and a profound listening
occurs. A deep and penetrating awareness develops and reveals many
aspects of who we are.

Wisdom does not come from any particular object, any particular
state. Suzuki Roshi has spoken of "nothing special." There is
nothing special in our mind, in our body, in the way things are
happening. All things which arise have the nature to pass away;
there is no special thing to attain or grasp at, nothing special to hold
on to. Whatever comes as part of the flow is fine. What is important
is the balance and clarity of mind. There is no special desirability in
having unusual experiences. Although extraordinary phenomena

may sometimes occur, they are all nothing special, all more things to observe, subject to the same laws of impermanence. What we want to do is to let go of everything, not to identify with any state whatsoever. To be free on all sides, not to be attached, even by golden chains, to anything that's happening. When we experience this flow of impermanence very deeply, when we have a clear and direct vision that every part of our being is in change, in transformation, then we begin to let go of our most deeply conditioned attachments, and we come into harmony with the flow. Not resisting, not holding on, not grasping. We become one with the unfolding of the Dharma.

Question: *Is there no soul, even as part of the process?*

Answer: The whole development of awareness comes from experiencing things with a silent mind, not with our thoughts and concepts about them. It's going from the thought-conceptual level of mind to the intuitive-experiential level. All the words that are used are irrelevant in comparison to the experience of silent awareness. I think what is worthy of mentioning now is that there is no need to blindly believe anything. The true deep understanding will come from your own experience in meditation. Whether or not you know the concepts does not matter. Some of the most advanced yogis never studied, never read a book, are not necessarily bright, but just take instruction in practice and do it. The whole Dharma unfolds within them; they experience many stages of enlightenment and yet may not have the words to communicate their silent understanding. What's most important is the experience of the truth within ourselves which is free of ideas and opinions.

What is the purpose of concentration practices?

There are different ways of developing the path. A very traditional way is to develop concentration first, and then use that power of mind to develop insight. This can take a long time because special circumstances are needed to develop strong concentration. Part of what happened in Burma, in particular, in the last 100 or 150 years is the revival of Vipassana techniques which develop mindfulness and concentration simultaneously, bringing together moment to moment awareness and concentration sufficient for enlightenment.

Is there any choice in what we do in this world?

Much of what happens to us is determined by our past karma, but how we react to it is very much within our freedom of the moment. We can cultivate mindfulness or not. There is no necessity binding us to react to things. Freedom lies in how we relate to what is happening in the moment.

How does western psychology's notion of a subconscious relate to meditation?

What happens as the mind becomes silent and we become more finely aware, is that many of the things which were below our normal threshold of awareness, much of what is called subconscious material, become illuminated by mindfulness. We begin to observe what was formerly subconscious conditioning, and through the awareness of it begin to integrate it more fully in our mind.

Does always trying to be aware in the moment lessen spontaneity?

Being unaware does not mean being spontaneous. If we're acting mechanically, very much as a conditioned response to phenomena, that's not spontaneity, that's being a robot. A certain input comes, we act, all the time unaware, unmindful. That is not a spontaneous state of mind—it's a mechanical one. Spontaneity comes when the mind is silent, when the mind is on the intuitive level, clearly noticing moment to moment. When mindfulness is developed, it does not chop up the flow, breaking the natural rhythm. In the beginning it may be useful to focus on each particular process, but when bare attention is cultivated, it flows along effortlessly.

With the analogy of practicing the piano and practicing bare attention, just as there are many people who practice the piano but very few who become adept, wouldn't that hold true for practicing bare attention, that very few people actually become mindful?

People progress in different ways. It's said that some people progress slowly and with a lot of pain. Others progress slowly but with mostly pleasant sensations. Some progress quickly with a lot of pain, and others progress quickly with a lot of pleasure. It very much depends on our past accumulations of karma, how developed our spiritual faculties of mind already are. But if we're facing in the right direction, all we have to do is keep on walking. If it takes a year, or sixty years, or five lifetimes, as long as we're heading towards light, that's all that matters. We want to be facing in the direction of freedom, not going backwards, not going towards more darkness. So whatever each person's evolution might be, where we are is where we have to start from.

You talk about somebody going through lifetimes. Is there something that goes through all those lifetimes like a soul?

It can be understood somewhat in terms of the changes that happen within a lifetime. For example, if you think back five or ten years, your body was completely different, even on a cellular level. It has all undergone transformation. The mind has undergone transformation countless more times, arising and passing away. There is nothing which you can point to now, nothing at all, in the mind and body, which is the same as it was then. But what you are now has been conditioned by what you were then and by every successive moment. In other words, every moment conditions the arising of the next moment. Nothing is carried over, but there is a relationship of one moment to the next. There is an ordered continuity to the process. At the moment of death, the quality of consciousness conditions the arising of the rebirth consciousness. Nothing is carried over, but depending on that last moment arises the new consciousness.

26

•

Instruction: Thoughts

It is important to make thoughts the object of mindfulness. If we remain unaware of thoughts as they arise, it is difficult to develop insight into their impersonal nature and into our own deep-rooted and subtle identification with the thought process. This identification reinforces the illusion of self, of some "one" who is thinking. To meditate upon thoughts is simply to be aware, as thoughts arise, that the mind is thinking, without getting involved in the content: not going off on a train of association, not analyzing the thought and why it came, but merely to be aware that at the particular moment "thinking" is happening. It is helpful to make a mental note of "thinking, thinking" every time a thought arises; observe the thought without judgment, without reaction to the content, without identifying with it, without taking the thought to be I, or self, or mine. The thought is the thinker. There is no one behind it. The thought is thinking itself. It comes uninvited. You will see that when there is a strong detachment from the thought process, thoughts don't last long. As soon as you are mindful of a thought, it disappears and the attention returns to the breath. Some people may find it helpful to label the thinking process in a more precise way, to note different kinds of thoughts, whether "planning" or "imagining" or "remembering." This sharpens the focus of attention. Otherwise, the simple note of "thinking, thinking" will serve the purpose. Try to be aware of the thought as soon as it arises, rather than some minutes afterward. When they are noticed with precision and balance they have no power to disturb the mind.

Thoughts should not be treated as obstacles or hindrances. They are just another object of mindfulness, another object of meditation. Don't let the mind become lazy and drift along. Make the effort for a great deal of clarity with respect to what's happening in the moment.

Suzuki Roshi in *Zen Mind, Beginner's Mind* writes:

When you are practicing Zazen meditation do not try to stop your thinking. Let it stop by itself. If something comes into your mind, let it come in and let it go out. It will not stay long. When you try to stop your thinking, it means you are bothered by it. Do not be bothered by anything. It appears that the something comes from outside your mind, but actually it is only the waves of your mind and if you are not bothered by the waves, gradually they will become calmer and calmer . . . Many sensations come, many thoughts or images arise but they are just waves from your own mind. Nothing comes from outside your mind . . . If you leave your mind as it is, it will become calm. This mind is called big mind.

Just let things happen as they do. Let all images and thoughts and sensations arise and pass away without being bothered, without reacting, without judging, without clinging, without identifying with them. Become one with the big mind, observing carefully, microscopically, all the waves coming and going. This attitude will quickly bring about a state of balance and calm. Don't let the mind get out of focus. Keep the mind sharply aware, moment to moment, of what is happening, whether the in-out breath, the rising-falling, sensations, or thoughts. In each instant be focused on the object with a balanced and relaxed mind.

28

•

Concepts and Reality

There is a famous parable in the *Republic* of Plato about a cave. In the cave is a row of people, chained in such a way that they can only face the back wall. Behind the row of people is a fire and a procession of figures walking by engaged in all the activities of life. The procession of figures casts shadows on the back wall of the cave. The people who are chained can see only the changing view of shadows, and because that is all they have ever seen, they take these shadows to be ultimate reality. Sometimes a person who is bound in this way, through great effort, manages to loosen the chains and turn around. He or she sees the fire and the procession and begins to understand that the shadows are not the reality, but merely a reflection on the wall. Perhaps with further effort that person is able to cut the chains completely and emerge into the sunlight, into freedom.

Our predicament is similar to those people chained in the cave. The shadows are the world of concepts in which we live. Chained through our attachments, we perceive the world through our ideas, our thoughts, our mental constructs, taking these concepts to be the reality itself.

There are many concepts with which we have been strongly conditioned, and which are deeply ingrained in our minds. For example, many people's lives are committed to the concept of place, of country, of nation. On the planet, there are no divisions between countries. Our minds have created these arbitrary divisions. Every time you cross a border you see how much "reality" has been invested in this concept of place. So many problems in the world—political and economic tensions and hostilities—are related to the thought, "This is *my* nation, *my* country." In understanding that the concept is only the product of our own thought processes, we can begin to free ourselves from that attachment.

A story illustrating concept of place was told to me by a Greek girl who was traveling to India. She described a border crossing in the middle of a desert. The border was a dry riverbed, and over the riverbed was a great iron bridge, half of which was painted green, the other half painted red. There was nothing around except barren desert and a multi-colored bridge. Just in the middle of the bridge was a big iron gate locked from both sides. When someone wanted to go from one "country" to the other, guards on one side of the bridge called to guards on the other side and, coming up to the center just at the same time, they turned their keys in the locks, and opened the gate: crossing the border!

Concepts of time are also strongly conditioned in our minds, ideas of past and future. What is it that we call time? We have certain thoughts occurring in the present moment—memories, reflections—we label this whole class of thoughts "past," and project it somewhere beyond us, apart from the present moment. Likewise, we engage in planning or imagining, label these thoughts "future," and project them outside into some imagined reality. We rarely see that "past" and "future" are happening right now. All that there is, is an unfolding of present moments. We have created these concepts to serve a useful purpose, but by taking the ideas to be the reality, by not understanding that they are merely the product of our own thought processes, we find ourselves burdened by worries and regrets about the past and anxieties of anticipation about what has not yet happened. When we can settle back into the moment, realizing that past and future are simply thoughts in the present, then we free ourselves from the bondage of "time."

It is useful to develop insight into the nature of concepts to see how attached we are to them. We have the idea that we "own" things. The cushion that we sit on does not know that it is owned by anyone. The concept of ownership deals with the relationship of nearness we have to various objects. At times we are near to objects, use them, and then have the idea that we own them. Actually, ownership is a thought process independent of the actual relationship that exists between us and objects in the world. Freeing ourselves from attachment to "ownership" frees us from our enslavement to objects.

Another concept with which we are all particularly involved is the concept of man and woman. When you close your eyes there is the breath, sensations, sounds, thoughts—where is "man" or "woman" except as an idea, a concept? Man and woman cease to exist when the mind is silent. Imagine waves arising out of the ocean and commenting upon each other as being big or small, beautiful or grand, which is true in a relative sense, but doesn't reflect the underlying unity of the great mass of water. It is just the same when we become attached to concepts about certain shapes and forms; comparisons, judgments, evaluations, all arise which strengthen the relative separateness and isolation. In meditation, we free ourselves from attachment to that conceptualization and experience the fundamental unity of the elements which comprise our being.

Perhaps the most deeply ingrained concept, the one that has kept us chained longest in the cave of shadows, binding us to the wheel of life and death and rebirth, is the concept of self. The idea that there is someone behind this flow, that there is some entity, some permanent element, which is the essence of our being. Self, I, me, mine are all ideas in the mind, arising out of our identification with various aspects of the mind-body process. From the beginning this "self" does not exist, yet because we're so firmly attached to the idea of it, we spend much of our lives defending or enlarging or satisfying this imaginary self. Meditation helps us to see its conceptual nature, to see that in reality it does not exist, that it is simply an idea, an extraneous projection onto what's happening in the moment.

These are a few of the concepts which keep us bound—concepts of place, of time, of ownership, of man or woman, of self. You can see how very strong these concepts are, how much of our lives revolve about them, how much we live in the world of shadow. Kalu Rinpoche, a well-known Tibetan meditation master, wrote,

> *"You live in illusion and the appearance of things. There is a Reality. You are that Reality. When you understand this, you will see that you are nothing. And being nothing, you are everything. That is all."*

There are four "ultimate realities." They are called that because they can be experienced, as opposed to merely thought about. These four ultimate realities are the entire content of our experience.

The first of these are the material elements composing all objects of the physical universe. Traditionally, and in terms of how we can experience them in our practice, they are described as the earth, air, fire and water elements. The earth element is the element of extension. We experience it as the hardness or softness of objects. When we experience pain in the body, it is a manifestation of this element. When we walk and have contact with the earth, that feeling of tangible contact is the earth element—the feeling of hardness, softness, extension.

The fire element is the quality of heat or cold. Sometimes in meditation the fire element may become very predominant and the body begins to feel as if it is burning. No "one" is burning, it is only the fire element manifesting its own nature; that is, the sensations of heat or cold.

The air element is vibration or movement. In the walking meditation, what we are experiencing is the play of elements. Foot and leg are concepts, a name we give to a certain way of experiencing the flow of elements. There is no foot, no leg, no body, no self; simply the experience of movement and touching sensations.

The water element represents fluidity and cohesion, the element responsible for holding things together. When you have dry flour, all the granules fall apart. They don't stick together. When you add water to it, then all those particles of flour cohere. That is how the water element manifests itself: holding all the material elements together.

Along with these four elements arise four secondary characteristics of matter—color, odor, taste, and nutritional qualty; the whole physical universe can be experienced in terms of these elements. We can become aware of them, free of thought about them. Floor does not exist; floor is a concept. What is experienced is the feeling of hardness or coldness or the color when we look at it. The eye sees color. It does not see a name. When walking out of doors, most people see "tree," but that's a conceptualization of what is seen. What is actually seen is color in a certain form. Another process of mind then labels that "tree." "Body" is a concept. When we are sitting in meditation, the "body" disappears. What is experienced is sensation: heat or cold or pain or tension, the workings of the elements only, all of which are impermanent, in constant transformation. The meditative experience allows us to begin to be aware on the experiential, non-conceptual level of things as they are, free of our thoughts about them. So that when we see something, we are aware of seeing color. When we feel something, we are aware of the qualities of the sensations without being attached to the concept, without always projecting some idea onto the experience.

It is interesting that concepts remain fixed while reality is always in flux. The word "body" stays the same but the body itself is everchanging. The concept is static but when we actually experience what is happening, we discover a flow of impermanent elements, an arising and passing away of sensations. The mindful experience of things reveals their true impermanent nature. As long as we are involved on a conceptual level, we maintain the illusion of permanence which keeps us bound to the wheel of life and death.

The process of developing insight and wisdom is to begin to experience the realities rather than the shadows. Then the true characteristics of nature become clear.

The second of the ultimate realities is consciousness. Consciousness is the knowing faculty, that which knows the object. Sometimes people have the idea that in this mind-body, there is one consciousness from birth to death, one observer who is knowing everything. This idea gives rise to the concept of a permanent self. It occurs when we have not silenced our minds enough to observe the flow of knowing. Consciousness itself is arising and passing away in each instant. There is not one mind which is observing all phenomena; at every instant "mind" is created and destroyed. The consciousness that hears is different from the consciousness that sees, or tastes, or smells, or touches, or thinks. There are different mind-moments, arising and passing away every instant. When the mind becomes quiet, it is possible to observe this flow of consciousness. Insight into the flow and impermanence of the knowing faculty, understanding that there is not one knower, one observer, but rather an ongoing process at every moment, exposes the illusion of a permanent self.

The third of the ultimate realities is called mental factors. They are the qualities of mind which determine how consciousness relates to the object. Different combinations of mental factors arise with each moment of consciousness and pass away with it. Greed, hatred and delusion are the three mental factors which are the roots of all unwholesome activity. All unwholesome karma, or action, is motivated by one or another of these three roots. For example, the factor of greed has the nature of clinging to an object. When greed arises in a moment of consciousness, it influences the mind in such a way that it clings, it sticks, it grasps, it is attached. That is the nature of the

34

greed factor. It is impermenent and not self, not I; merely a factor of mind working in its own way.

Hatred is a mental factor which has the nature of condemning the object, of having aversion. Aversion, ill will, annoyance, irritation. anger, all of these are expressions of the mental factor of hatred. Hatred is also not I, not self, not mine; it is an impermanent factor which arises and passes away.

Delusion is a factor which has the function of clouding the mind so that we are unaware of what the object is. We don't know what is happening.

There are also three wholesome roots of mind: non-greed, non-hatred, non-delusion. Non-greed has the nature of generosity, non-attachment, non-possessiveness. Non-hatred is love, feeling good will for all beings, friendship. Non-delusion is wisdom. Wisdom has the function of seeing clearly. It is like a light in the mind. If you go into a dark room, you can't see and you start stumbling over everything. If a light is put on, then all of the objects become distinct and clear. This is the function of wisdom: il-luminating the mind so we can see clearly both the content and process of our mind and body.

All of these mental factors are impersonal and impermanent. There is no one who is greedy, no one who is hateful, no one who is wise, no one who is generous. There is only the arising and passing of moments of consciousness concurrent with certain factors of mind, each one functioning in its own way. Where then does the idea of self come from? Why is it that we're so conditioned to believe in the existence of "I"?

There is one mental factor which is called "wrong view," and it has the function of identifying with the various changing elements of the mind and body. When the factor of wrong view occurs in a moment of consciousness, the concept of self arises. But it too is impermanent and impersonal, arising at times and passing away. When we are mindful in the moment, wrong view does not arise and so we begin to free ourselves from the conditioning of "I, me, mine." Every moment of mindfulness is a moment of egolessness, of purity.

The question has often been asked in this practice, "Who's being mindful?" Mindfulness, too, is a mental factor. It has the function of noticing what the object is, staying aware of the present moment. Gurdjieff called this quality self-remembering. There is no one who is mindful, only the functioning of a particular factor: an awareness without clinging, condemning or identifying. As mindfulness is developed, there is a deeper understanding that all conditioned phenomena are transitory and empty of an abiding self.

We are like a big, moving jigsaw puzzle. The pieces of the puzzle are the material elements, consciousness and mental factors. When the pieces join together in a certain way we see "man" or "woman," "tree," "house." But that is only the *picture* of the arranged pieces, the concepts. It is the fundamental elements of mind and body, the underlying energies in constant flow and transformation, which constitute the reality of our experience.

The fourth ultimate reality is nirvana. Nirvana is like the experience of a person freeing himself entirely from the chains and emerging from the cave into sunlight, going beyond this conditioned mind-body process into freedom.

All of these ultimate realities can be experienced. The words we use to describe them are concepts which merely point to the experience. The meditation practice develops awareness of them beyond the words. We are all in the process of breaking the chains that keep us bound in the cave of ignorance. At times during the practice it may seem as if nothing much is happening except a lot of pain and restlessness and agitation and doubt. But, in fact, every moment of awareness, every moment of mindfulness helps to weaken the chain of our attachments. We are building the momentum of that awareness and, as the mindfulness and concentration get stronger, the mind becomes more powerful and insightful. Very patiently, we begin to experience what this mind-body process is all about, experiencing it free of concepts; free of the idea of self; emerging from the darkness of the cave into the light of freedom and peace.

Question: *How did we get from ultimate reality to conceptual thinking? How did we get so far away from this simple process that we should all be experiencing?*

Answer: It's not as if we have fallen from a state of purity into a state of delusion. Ignorance and desire are the two causes which have kept us going from beginningless time: ignorance and desire driving us around this wheel of rebirth. The fact that we are in this state now is the dilemma and the problem that confronts us. There is a way out, which is to eliminate ignorance and craving. And that's done by paying attention to what is happening on the experiential level.

How can we live in the world without concepts?

Please understand that concepts should be used. It's not that once we experience a reality beyond the conceptual level we throw out the whole intellectual process. We have to use that process of mind in dealing successfully with the world, in living our lives. There are two levels of truth: one is conventional truth in which we use all these concepts of "man" and "woman" and "I" and "time" and "place." The other is ultimate truth which deals with the four realities. We can use concepts without being a slave to them. We should understand they are only conventional truth and that there is an underlying reality. In Bodhgaya, which is where many of us studied in India, there was an elephant. Often the elephant would be walking down the road as we would be going into town. We would be walking mindfully, really slowly, paying attention. When we saw the elephant coming down the road we did not just stand there saying "seeing, seeing," we moved out of the way. Use the thought process when appropriate.

What are emotions?

Emotions are different mental factors. Anger, jealousy, compassion, joy and love are mental factors. All emotions are impersonal qualities of mind. There's no one behind them. No one who is angry, no one who is loving—simply factors functioning in their own way.

What conditions the arising of mindfulness?

Wisdom, or seeing clearly the nature of our conditioning and understanding the way to freedom. The effort factor becomes a cause for mindfulness to arise. Faith or confidence, too, can be the condition for arousing the effort to be mindful.

Can you say something about love?

The expression of emptiness is love, because emptiness means "emptiness of self." When there is no self, there is no other. That duality is created by the idea of self, of I, of ego. When there's no self, there is a unity, a communion. And without the thought of "I'm loving someone," love becomes the natural expression of that oneness.

When you are mindful of consciousness, what is being mindful?

Mindfulness is a mental factor which has as its function remembering what the object is, not allowing the mind to forget. The mindfulness can be turned toward the object or it can be turned toward the consciousness, the knowing of it. Generally, it's easier to observe the object because it's more tangible. When the mind is very quiet you can also observe the knowing faculty arising and passing away. At that point it gets interesting because then we break our identification with consciousness, with knowing, as being I, which is a very subtle identification. It's easy to sit back and watch the flow of things and still have the idea of an observer doing it. But actually there isn't an observer at all. There is just knowing, arising and passing away every moment. Knowing or consciousness is a process also. It's impermanent, impersonal, not I, not self.

What is memory? Where does it fit in?

Memory is a complicated working of certain mental factors, mostly involved with perception. Perception is the mental factor which has the function of recognition, to pick out the distinguishing characteristics of an object. It is through the mental factor of perception that we recognize from the experience of previous mind moments what an object is. Memory is a class of thoughts which takes as its object something already experienced.

Where does an individual's propensity towards a particular type of behavior come from?

The continual repetition or practice of certain kinds of volitions create tendencies. Right now we are strengthening mindfulness, concentration and insight, and developing a tendency towards wisdom and understanding. Likewise, in the past, through the repetition of certain kinds of volitions and actions we have created all our different personalities, all our tendencies to do certain things. Personality can be understood in terms of these inherent tendencies. There is no one thing which is the personality, though a certain mental factor can be predominant at times. In a person who cultivates greed, who continually practices clinging and grasping, attachment and forgetfulness, the greed factor becomes very strong in the mind. Soon it is expressed in all of his actions. When non-greed or non-hatred is cultivated, then it becomes the predominant tendency and is expressed in the personality.

Where does the factor of will come in?

Choice is another mental factor. There is an intricate interconnection between all the different factors of mind. Choice is there, the whole decision making process is there, effort is there. They express their own natures and functions. One of the proximate causes for establishing mindfulness is said to be the hearing of the teaching, the Dharma. That becomes the cause for the factor of effort to arise. The Buddha spoke very often about the great skill in coming to hear

39

the Dharma. It arouses the effort factor to begin establishing mindfulness. The mental factors, including "will," are all latent in the mind. We don't have to do anything to create the factors. It is just a question of which factors are going to be cultivated. Certain decisions come from hearing the Dharma, understanding what it's all about. That motivates the arising of effort to develop mindfulness and awareness, to develop insight and wisdom. There's a stanza in the Dhammapada which says, "There is acting without an actor, there is doing without a doer, there is suffering without anyone who suffers, there is enlightenment without anyone who gets enlightened."

What is the intellect?

The intellect is the thought-conceptual level of the mind. It can be trained, developed, and used; or it can be a hindrance. It depends how clearly we understand the thought process. If there's clear insight into its nature, it's not a hindrance at all. If we mistake the thoughts about things for the things themselves, it becomes an obstacle in that it confuses concept with reality. But, in itself, it's just another part of the entire mind-body process. There is a line from the third Zen Patriarch: "Do not dislike even the world of senses and ideas. Indeed, to accept them fully is identical with true enlightenment."

•

Instruction: Sense Objects

When visual images arise in the practice, simply make a note of "seeing, seeing," without getting involved in judging or evaluating the content. Just observe the arising and passing away of the images. When sounds become predominant, make a note of "hearing, hearing," not analyzing or conceptualizing its causes. If some smell or odor should become noticeable, make a note of "smelling, smelling," and again go back to the breathing. The more closely you pay attention to the primary object, the more quickly will the mind pick up all other objects.

SEVENTH
AFTERNOON

•

Stories

The way to develop a strong momentum of awareness is to increase the frequency of noticing. In the beginning of the practice, you notice at rather long intervals, first one object and a bit later, another. The practice develops by increasing this frequency of noticing objects, so that it becomes instant to instant, picking up in each moment the different objects, the flow of the breath, or sensations in the body, or thoughts. Being with the flow of phenomena on a microscopic level is the kind of mindfulness that develops with practice. The Buddha gave an example of just how mindful we should be. He told of a person who was ordered to walk through a very crowded marketplace with a water jug full to the brim balanced on his head. Behind him walked a soldier with a big sword. If a single drop of that water were to fall, the soldier would cut off his head. Assuredly, the person with the jug walked pretty mindfully. But it has to be mindful in an easy way. If there is too much forcing or strain, the least little jostling will cause the water to spill. The person with the jug has to be loose and rhythmic, flowing with the changing scene, yet staying very attentive in each moment. That is the kind of care we should take in developing awareness: a relaxed alertness.

A certain effort is involved in developing this moment to moment awareness. It is not the effort to attain anything in the future. The effort is to stay just in the present, in paying attention with equanimity to what is happening in the moment.

There is a story about someone who had been practicing for some time going to visit a Zen master. It was raining, and as he went in the door, he left his shoes and umbrella outside. After he paid his respects, the master asked him on which side of his shoes he had left his umbrella. He couldn't remember. It is said that he went away for seven more years to perfect his moment to moment Zen.

It's important to develop a steady penetrating awareness with regard to everything we do, from the time of waking up in the morning to the time of going to sleep. Just upon awakening be aware of "rising-falling," or "in-out," and from that first moment, be mindful of the actions involved in getting up and washing, beginning to walk, going to sit and then in standing again and going for food. In lying down to sleep, be with the "rising-falling," or "in-out," until the last moment before sleep. This kind of attention will be of great benefit in the meditation practice. If there is the idea that the practice is only sitting and walking, and the rest of the time is not important, then in all those breaks we lose the momentum that has been building. Cultivating a strong awareness in every action throughout the day helps the mind to remain concentrated and still. It is this kind of determination and balance of mind out of which enlightenment happens.

There is no circumstance at all which we should consider unworthy of awareness. The sudden deep intuition of truth can happen in a moment, when all the factors of enlightenment ripen and come together in the right balance.

There is a story about Ananda, who was personal attendant to the Buddha, taking care of all his needs and arranging everything for him. But in serving as attendant to the Buddha, he did not have much time to practice. His friends were all becoming fully enlightened and he remained at the beginning stage. Only after the Buddha died did he have a chance to resume intensive practice. Sometime after the Buddha's death, the monks called together a big council to recite all the discourses of the Buddha so that they would not be forgotten. They selected 499 monks, all of whom were fully enlightened with full psychic powers, and Ananda. They selected Ananda because he had been present every time the Buddha had given a talk and because he had the power of perfect recall. So although he wasn't fully enlightened, he was a valuable asset to the council. As the day of the meeting came near, the monks all urged Ananda to intensify his practice. On the night before the big council Ananda was really making a strenuous effort. He was doing the walking meditation, "lifting, forward, placing." Midnight, one, two in the morning and still nothing had happened. At four in the morning, Ananda took stock of the situation. He was a very wise man and had heard all of the Buddha's teaching. He recognized that his mind was out of balance. He was making too much effort without sufficient concentration and tranquility. There was too much expectation and anticipation in his mind. So he thought to lie down and meditate, trying to bring those factors into balance. Very mindfully, he went to his bed, watching the whole process. And it is said that just as his head was about to touch the pillow, before his feet had been set on the bed, in that instant, he experienced the highest truth, and that with his liberation also came all the psychic powers. It was then four in the morning and until six or seven he enjoyed the bliss of nirvana, of peace. In the morning, he appeared spontaneously in his place at the meeting and everybody realized that Ananda had made it.

There's no knowing when the clouds of ignorance will be dispelled. It can happen even in the process of lying down to sleep. Be mindful! In every single moment, be watchful, awake to what's happening. This kind of practice, day after day, builds an extraordinary strength of mind. Use the opportunity of this retreat to the fullest: don't waste time or think you've done enough. If late in the evening you do not feel sleepy, continue the practice. Often the late night hours are the best for meditation. There should be the greatest effort possible without forcing, without creating tension.

When I was in India and I first began practicing, there was a friend who lived across the hall. He was the perfect model of perseverance. Every time I saw him, he was meditating. When it came ten or eleven at night, I was ready to go to sleep. But I would see his light on and feel encouraged to continue, so I would get up from the sitting and walk for some time. After walking, my mind and body became energized, and again I could sit for an hour or two. I would sit and walk and sit. In that way, I pushed myself as far as possible, and it was very valuable. There is a cumulative effect of concentration and mindfulness so that by the end of a day of practice, in the night hours, the mind achieves a very penetrating quality. If you feel that happening, please continue the practice. Sit and walk as much as possible. There are many things to experience, many levels of mind to experience.

In many of the meditation centers in Burma, yogis begin with four hours of sleep and, as the meditation develops, need less and less. We should not fall into the trap of our conditioning, thinking that if we don't get seven or eight hours of sleep we're going to be exhausted. That is simply an old habit pattern. When the mind is balanced all day, not clinging, not condemning, not identifying with things, we don't accumulate much fatigue or tension. My teacher said that when he trained in Burma he went through a period of five days without sleeping, not feeling tired at all. Just working rhythmically and evenly, doing this very same practice of Vipassana, the practice of mindfulness. Stay sensitive to your changing needs and if you're not feeling tired or sleepy, continue the practice through the night.

•

Instruction: Intentions

Volition is a common factor of mind present in every moment of consciousness. When it is predominant, it should be noticed. Volition is the mental urge or signal which precedes any action. When we are mindful of volitions and intentions, we then have the freedom to choose whether or not we want to act on them. As long as we remain unaware of intentions, actions will follow automatically. For example, when you are sitting in meditation, before you stand up, there is an intention to stand. When you notice the intention, which will arise and pass away, you will perhaps go on sitting, because you have been mindful of it, not identifying with it. If the intention arises without mindfulness, we find ourselves standing, without having been aware at all of the process involved. It is that way with all voluntary movements of the body. So when intentions are predominant, as they are between radical changes of posture, between sitting and standing, standing and walking, be mindful of them. In walking, there is an intention to stop before stopping. There is an intention to turn before turning. There is no need to single out the intention with each step, but it is helpful to notice it when you come to the end of your walk, just as you are beginning to turn. The foot by itself does not make that turning movement. It turns because of a preceding volition. A lot of insight into the cause and effect relationship of mind and body develops through this kind of observation. Sometimes the body is the cause and a mind-state is the effect. Sometimes the mind is the cause and a body movement is the effect. An intention arises to turn and the leg moves. There is no one there, no one "doing" the turning. It is an impersonal cause and effect relationship. But, if in starting to turn we are unmindful of how it is that the process is happening, it becomes easy to identify with the idea that there's some "one" who is doing it.

Suppose you are feeling cold and you go to put on a sweater. Because of physical sensation, desire arises for greater warmth. Because of the desire, intention arises to get more clothing. Because of intention, the body starts to move. Becoming mindful of these intentions causes insight into the interrelated way mind-body processes are working.

In sitting, intentions will be noticeable before each movement. If you change position, there will be an intention to do so. If you swallow, there will be a preceding intention. If you open your eyes, there will be an intention to open. All of these should be noticed. Intentions are not always thoughts in the mind, not always words. Sometimes they are experienced just as an urge, a signal that something is about to happen. You need not be looking for words or a sentence in the mind. Just be aware of that impulse to do something. And as you begin to notice how this cause and effect relationship is working in the mind and body, the concept of self dissolves into a simple and natural unfolding of the elements.

•

Instruction: Eating

There are many different processes of mind and body which go on while we eat. It is important to become mindful of the sequence of the processes; otherwise, there is a great likelihood of greed and desire arising with regard to food. And when we are not aware, we do not fully enjoy the experience. We take a bite or two and our thoughts wander.

The first process involved when you have your food is that you see it. Notice "seeing, seeing." Then there is an intention to take the food, a mental process. That intention should be noticed. "Intending, intending." The mental intention becomes the cause of the arm moving. "Moving, moving." When the hand or spoon touches the food there is the sensation of touch, contact. Feel the sensations. Then the intention to lift the arm, and the lifting. Notice carefully all these processes.

Opening the mouth. Putting in the food. Closing the mouth. The intention to lower the arm, and then the movement. One thing at a time. Feeling the food in the mouth, the texture. Chewing. Experience the movement. As you begin chewing, there will be taste sensations arising. Be mindful of the tasting. As you keep on chewing, the taste disappears. Swallowing. Be aware of the whole sequence involved. There is no one behind it, no one who is eating. It's merely the sequence of intentions, movements, tastes, touch sensations. That's what we are—a sequence of happenings, of processes, and by being very mindful of the sequence, of the flow, we get free of the concept of self. We see this whole working of mind and body as a continuity of processes. Intentions, thoughts, sensations, movements, all in interrelationship to one another, the mind being the cause of bodily movements, bodily sensations being the cause of desires and intentions in the mind.

Usually we eat very unmindfully. Taste comes and goes very quickly. While food is still in the mouth, because of desire and greed for continuing taste sensations, the arm reaches for more, and generally we are unaware of the whole process involved. Finish each mouthful before reaching for another. In this way we become sensitive to our bodies and how much food we need. It's very hard to overeat when you eat mindfully.

In this month of training, everything is slowed down so we have the chance to carefully examine what's happening. When mindfulness is well developed, you can do things quickly as well. But this is a time for training. There is no hurry. Do everything slowly, with silence and awareness. Incorporate the eating meditation into your daily practice so there is no gap in the continuity of awareness. From the moment you get up, through everything done in the day, be very mindful, make it all meditation.

•

Hindrances

Imagine yourselves in the middle of a battlefield, single-handedly facing a thousand enemies. Though surrounded on all sides, you somehow manage to conquer them. Imagine yourself on this battlefield a thousand different times, and each time you overcome the enemies around you. The Buddha has said that this is an easier task than the conquering of oneself. It is not a trivial thing we have set about doing. The most difficult of all possible tasks is to come to understand one's own mind. But it is not impossible. There have been many beings who have conquered these thousand enemies a thousand times, and they have given us advice and guidance.

The first big help is to recognize who the enemies are. Unrecognized, they remain powerful forces in the mind; in the light of recognition, they become much easier to deal with. There are five powerful enemies in the battlefield of the mind and learning to recognize them is essential in penetrating to deeper levels of understanding.

The first of these enemies, or hindrances, is sense desire: lusting after sense pleasure, grasping at sense objects. It keeps the mind looking outward, searching after this object or that, in an agitated and unbalanced way. It is in the very nature of sense desires that they can never be satisfied. There is no end to the seeking. We enjoy a pleasurable object, it arises and disappears, as do all phenomena, and we are left with the same unsatiated desire for more gratification. Until we deal with that kind of grasping in the mind we remain always unfulfilled, always seeking a new pleasure, a new delight. It can be desires for beautiful sights, beautiful sounds, tastes or smells, pleasant sensations in the body, or fascinating ideas. Attachment to these objects strengthens the greed factor; and it is precisely greed in the mind, this clinging and grasping, which keeps us bound on the wheel of samsara, the wheel of life and death. Until we deal successfully with the hindrance of sense desire, we stay bound by the forces of attachment and possessiveness.

The second enemy is hatred; anger, ill will, aversion, annoyance, irritation, are all expressions of the condemning mind. It is the mind which strikes against the object and wants to get rid of it. It is a very turbulent and violent state. In English we use two expressions which clearly indicate the effect of these two enemies, sense desire and ill will. We say a person is "burning with desire," or a person is "burning up," to mean he or she is very angry. The mind in these states is literally burning: a great deal of suffering.

The third enemy is sloth and torpor, which means laziness of mind, sluggishness. A mind that is filled with sloth and torpor wants just to go to sleep. There is an animal called a slug which has always represented to me this quality of sloth and torpor: it barely inches along, rather unergetically. Unless we overcome that kind of drowsiness and sluggishness of mind, nothing gets done, nothing is seen clearly, our mind remains heavy and dull.

The fourth hindrance is restlessness. A mind that is in a state of worry, regret and agitation is unable to stay concentrated. It is always jumping from one object to another, without any mindfulness. This unsettledness of mind prevents the arising of deep insight.

52

The fifth of the great enemies is doubt, and in some ways it is the most difficult of all. Until we see through it, doubt incapacitates the mind, blocking our effort for clarity. Doubt arises about what one is doing and about one's ability to do it. Perhaps since you've been here the thought has come, "What am I doing here? Why did I come? I can't do it, it's too hard." This is the doubting mind, a very big obstacle on the path.

All of these hindrances—desire, anger, sloth and torpor, restlessness, doubt—are mental factors. They are not self, just impersonal factors functioning in their own way. A simile is given to illustrate the effect of these different obstructions in the mind. Imagine a pond of clear water. Sense desire is like the water becoming colored with pretty dyes. We become entranced with the beauty and intricacy of the color and so do not penetrate to the depths. Anger, ill will, aversion, is like boiling water. Water that is boiling is very turbulent. You can't see through to the bottom. This kind of turbulence in the mind, the violent reaction of hatred and aversion, is a great obstacle to understanding. Sloth and torpor is like the pond of water covered with algae, very dense. One cannot possibly penetrate to the bottom because you can't see through the algae. It is a very heavy mind. Restlessness and worry are like a pond when wind-swept. The surface of the water is agitated by strong winds. When influenced by restlessness and worry, insight becomes impossible because the mind is not centered or calm. Doubt is like the water when muddied; wisdom is obscured by murkiness and cloudiness.

There are specific ways to deal with these enemies as they confront us on the path. The first is to recognize them, to see them clearly in each moment. If sense desire arises, to know immediately that there is desire in the mind, or if there is anger, or sloth, or restlessness, or doubt, to recognize immediately the particular obstacle that has arisen. That very recognition is the most powerful, most effective way of overcoming them. Recognition leads to mindfulness. And mindfulness means not clinging, not condemning, not identifying with the object. All the hindrances are impermanent mental factors. They arise and they pass away, like clouds in the sky. If we are mindful of them when they arise and don't react or identify with them, they pass through the mind, without creating any disturbance. Mindfulness is the most effective way of dealing with them.

There are also specific antidotes to these hindrances when the mind becomes somewhat overpowered by them and mindfulness is still weak. When sense desire overcomes the mind, it is good to reflect upon the true nature of this decaying body, the fact that we are all going to end as corpses. In what may seem just a moment's time, we will be seventy or eighty or ninety years old. Han Shan, an ancient Chinese recluse and poet, perceived this clearly:

> *A curtain of pearls hangs before the hall of jade,*
> *And within is a lovely lady,*
> *Fairer in form than the gods and immortals,*
> *Her face like a blossom of peach or plum.*
> *Spring mists will cover the eastern mansion,*
> *Autumn winds blow from the western lodge,*
> *And after thirty years have passed,*
> *She will look like a piece of pressed sugar cane.*

This kind of reflection weakens lust as we realize the imminence of our own death. It's not that death is for some and not for others. We do not feel the uniqueness and power of the moment when we do not feel the urgency of our death.

There is also a strong correlation between the degree of desire we experience and over-indulgence in food and sleep. Moderation in eating and sleeping weakens the factor of desire and brings greater clarity.

Ill will, anger, aversion, hatred; again, the best way of dealing with these hindrances is to be aware of them, to be mindful. You are sitting and all of a sudden are filled with ill will towards a person or situation. Sit back and notice, "anger, anger." Not identifying with it, not condemning oneself for being angry. Simply watch. It arises and passes away. Anger is strong when it is fed with identification, "I'm angry and I should be angry because someone did something to me. . . ." As an alternative to the indulgence of expressing ill will, just closely observe it. You will find that it loses its power to disturb the mind. A specific way of dealing with ill will when it is too overpowering is to generate loving thoughts: wishing happiness and love to all beings everywhere, to individual people you feel very kindly towards, and finally to the specific person you may be angry at, surrounding that person with loving thoughts even though at the time it may be difficult. Slowly the anger will dissipate and the mind will again become cool and balanced. A very practical way of dealing with ill will, if you are feeling very strong aversion towards someone, is to give them a gift. It is hard to stay angry in the act of giving and, because you are being generous and open, it helps to dissolve the tensions and irritations that were there. It is a skillful way of freeing the mind from the fire of hatred.

Perhaps an even more insightful way of dealing with anger and aversion is to reflect upon the law of karma: to understand that we are all the heirs of our own actions. Every being is going to experience the results of his wholesome and unwholesome deeds. If somebody is doing something unwholesome, instead of reacting with anger, we can respond with compassion, understanding that the person is acting out of ignorance, in a way that will bring back pain and suffering to himself. There is no need to add to the suffering he is causing for himself; rather, out of compassion, we should try to ease that burden of ignorance.

Sloth and torpor. Again, the very best way of dealing with it is to observe it carefully, examining and investigating the qualities of sloth and torpor and sluggishness in the mind. Penetrate into it. With this kind of investigating mindfulness you can often experience all the sleepiness, all the drowsiness disappearing in just a moment. You can be noticing for some time "sleepy, sleepy," and then in a moment, the mind will become fully awake and mindful. By paying attention and not identifying with the feeling of sleepiness, it will usually pass away. But if you try being mindful and keep nodding off anyway, there are some specific things to do. Change posture. If you're sitting, get up and do some brisk walking. Or if you're inside, go outside. Being in the fresh air energizes one again. Look at a light for a few moments, either an electric light, moonlight, or starlight. The effect of light awakens the system. Throw cold water on yourself. Try walking backwards. Sloth and torpor are impermanent and can be overcome. If you have done all these things and are still nodding off, then it is time to go to sleep. But make the effort. If every time drowsiness comes into the mind we think, "Oh well, I'll take a little nap," it makes the factor of sloth stronger. Be resolute and energetic in dealing with this hindrance.

Restlessness and agitation. Again, be mindful of it. Look at the restless mind, examine what that mind is all about, pay close attention to the quality of restlessness. If you're sitting and are feeling agitated and not concentrated, make that mental state the object of awareness. Just sit and watch, "restless, restless." Observe without identifying with it. There is no "one" who is restless; rather it is the working of a particular mental factor. It comes and goes. If there is a balanced awareness, it does not disturb the mind.

Another way is to make the effort to concentrate the mind, to make the mind one-pointed. This is the specific antidote to restlessness. If the mind is feeling very agitated, return to the awareness of the breath. Give the mind a single object and stay with that object for a period of time, twenty minutes, half an hour, so that the factor of concentration becomes strong again. Sitting motionless in a very straight and precise posture also helps to overcome restlessness.

The last of the enemies is doubt. It is essential to see what doubt is all about because it can be an impenetrable barrier on the path. One just gives up. Again, the most effective and insightful way of dealing with doubt is to look at it, to face it, to acknowledge it. When doubt is present, pay full attention to the doubting mind, without identifying with it. Doubt is not self, not mine, and not I. It is merely a thought, a mental factor. If we can see it and not identify with it, the doubt comes, we sit back and notice, "doubting, doubting," and it goes away.

Another way of dealing with doubt is to have a good conceptual understanding of what is that we're doing, what the whole path of insight is about. There is no need for any kind of blind faith or acceptance. Understanding the Dharma on the intellectual level can be a great help in resolving doubts as they arise. Then when doubt comes you are able to clarify it from your own experience, your own understanding.

Often there is a tendency to condemn the hindrances when they arise. The condemning mind is itself the factor of aversion. Every act of condemning the hindrances strengthens the enemy. That's not the way. No judging, no evaluating. The hindrances come, simply observe them. Mindfulness makes them all inoperative. They may continue to arise, but they do not disturb the mind because we are not reacting to them.

As long as the hindrances remain strong in the mind, it is difficult to develop insight and wisdom. In the first few days, there was a lot of restlessness, doubt, and desire, until the mind began to settle down. The difficulties at the beginning are not the enemies' last stand. They will arise again as the mind begins to penetrate into deeper levels of conditioning. But now there should be some confidence in your ability to deal with these factors, having seen them come and go, arise and vanish. The understanding that they are impermanent gives a strong balance to the mind. Please sustain the effort and continuity of awareness; the mind which has overcome the power of the hindrances is quite unshakeable in its balance and pliability.

Question: *What should I do when I am getting uptight from trying too hard?*

Answer: When you feel too much tension or forcing in the practice go outside and look at the trees, look at the sky. It's so beautiful here, so expansive. Go outside and walk around a bit in a more relaxed way, but still with awareness of what you are doing. In a short time, the place itself will cool the mind. The Buddha often recommended being in nature because of its tranquility for the mind.

Sometimes I am not able to notice the breathing process. What should I do?

When the mind becomes calm, the breath becomes fine. If you lose awareness of the breath completely, be with the awareness of bodily sensations, or the body posture, or just the awareness of knowing, even if there does not seem to be any particular object. When the concentration gets well developed, you sometimes lose all sense of the body. Stay mindful of that. It too is impermanent. The breath comes back.

What about when you recognize fear and try to figure out where it comes from?

You can do that, but it's an endless process. Analyzing the cause is not letting go. It is going to arise again and again, and each time you'll have to analyze the new causes. When insight is developed you can see a fear and let go of it. We don't have to figure out the causes of our problems, we have to let go of them. The meditative state of mind is the most basic way of dealing with these kinds of negativities. Seeing them, acknowledging them, not identifying with them, and letting them go. It's so simple. It just takes mindfulness, awareness of what is happening in the moment.

I keep identifying with all the hindrances. What is a skillful means for remedying this?

The Tibetans use an image I have found helpful. They liken the mind to a great clear sky, a cloudless sky. All the phenomena of mind and body are happenings in this clear sky. They are not the sky itself. The sky is clear and unaffected by what is happening. The clouds come and go, the winds come and go, the rain and sunlight all come and go, but the sky remains clear. Make the mind like a big clear sky and let everything arise and vanish on its own. Then the mind stays balanced, relaxed, observing the flow.

•

Instruction: Consciousness

One of the foundations of mindfulness is consciousness, the knowing faculty. One way to develop mindfulness of knowing is to treat consciousness itself as the object of meditation. In any movement of the body, you can begin to sense the knowing faculty because the physical object is so apparent. Relax the mind and try to sense the knowing faculty arising at the same time as the movement. It is important to remember that knowing and the object arise simultaneously. You cannot separate consciousness from the object. But it is possible to distinguish the two processes, to see that the flow of objects is one process and the flow of consciousness is another. They are happening simultaneously, with two different functions. The function of consciousness is to know. For example, when we are walking, the leg or foot does not know anything. It is merely the material elements working, heaviness or lightness which is the earth element, or movement which is the air element. The knowing of these elements is the mind, or consciousness. There's moving and the knowing. Simultaneous with the movement is the knowing of it. Do not try to pinpoint the consciousness, to precisely define it or limit it. It is a very subtle, immaterial object. But with a relaxed mind, we can begin to sense the process of consciousness. Because it is so subtle an object, it will force the mind to be very attentive. It is impossible to experience clearly if the mind is lax or lazy.

Sometimes in sitting you might turn the attention to the knowing. The breath experienced as the in-out or rising-falling, is a material process only. The knowing of it is the mind, consciousness. When you are silent and centered, turn the mindfulness toward the "knowing." Don't strain to find it or try to locate it somewhere in the body. Simply be aware in an easy way of the knowing process going on.

One of the factors of enlightenment is investigation of the Dharma, which means that investigative quality of the mind which examines, which explores, just how the elements of mind and body work. Don't be afraid to use the mind in that way, to investigate. But not with words, not with thoughts, not with concepts. Try to get a feel, a sense of the process of consciousness happening together with the object. This experience brings freedom from identification with the observer. Insight comes from the realization that observation is going on without an observer, witnessing without a witness.

•

Warrior

In the books by Carlos Castaneda, Don Juan speaks of the necessity for a man or woman of knowledge to live like a warrior. The image of being a warrior resonates deeply with the experiences of meditation. A warrior takes everything in life to be a challenge, responding fully to what happens without complaint or regret. What usually matters most to people is affirmation or certainty in the eyes of others; what matters most to a warrior is impeccability in one's own eyes. Impeccability means living with precision and a totality of attention. What we're doing in coming to an understanding of ourselves is the noblest thing that can be done. It is the eradication from the mind of greed, of hatred, of delusion; establishing in ourselves wisdom and loving compassion. It's difficult and rare and requires great impeccability. This does not necessarily entail going off to the Mexican desert or to a cave in the Himalayas. It means, rather, cultivating qualities of mind which bring about totality and wakefulness in every moment.

The book *Siddhartha* by Hermann Hesse, describes very beautifully the emergence of a warrior in a context quite different than that of Carlos and Don Juan. Siddhartha said that his training had left him with three powers: he could think, he could wait, he could fast. Three qualities of mind, three characteristics of a warrior. The ability to think in this sense means clarity, not being muddled or confused about what is happening. Clarity with respect to the body—being aware of postures, the breath, the interplay of the physical elements, becoming sensitive to just how much food and sleep is actually needed. Bringing all the different kinds of bodily energies into balance. Clarity with respect to the mind—emotions, thoughts, and different mental states. Not getting caught up in the whirlings of the mind, staying clear and balanced in their flow.

Another aspect of Siddhartha's power to think involves courage: not being locked into preconceptions of how things are. Courageous enough to be open and receptive to different possibilities. Siddhartha did not believe blindly. He didn't believe his friends or parents, not his teachers, nor even the Buddha. He wanted to find the truth for himself, and the courage to do that opened him to a wide range of experience; going into the forest for three years and practicing the ascetic disciplines; having a beautiful love relationship with Kamala, the courtesan; getting involved in the world of business and commerce. He was open and courageous enough to experience and accept all the consequences, and was not made timid by narrow thought distinctions. The power of thinking is the power of clarity and courage—to experiment, to investigate, to probe what's going on.

The courage of a warrior is both required and developed in the practice of meditation. It takes courage to sit with pain, without avoiding or masking it; just to sit and face it totally and overcome one's fear. It takes courage to probe and by that probing discover the deepest elements of the mind and body. It can be quite unsettling at first because many of our comfortable habits get overturned. It takes a lot of courage to let go of everything that we've been holding onto for security. To let go, to experience the flow of impermanence. It takes courage to face and confront the basic and inherent insecurity of this mind-body process. To confront the fact that in every instant what we are is continually dissolving, vanishing; that there is no place to take a stand at all. It takes courage to die. To experience the death of the concept of self; to experience that death while we're living takes the courage and fearlessness of an impeccable warrior.

Siddhartha could think and wait and fast.

Waiting means patience and silence. It means not being driven to action by our desires. If we don't have the ability to wait, every desire which comes into our minds compels us to action and we stay bound on the wheel of craving. Sometimes waiting is misinterpreted as inaction, not doing anything. It's not that at all. Chuang Tzu wrote,

> *The non-action of the wise man is not inaction. It is not studied. It is not shaken by anything. The sage is quiet because he is not moved, not because he wills to be quiet. Still water is like glass . . . it is a perfect level. If water is so clear, so level, how much more the spirit of man. The heart of the wise man is tranquil, it is the mirror of heaven and earth, the glass of everything. Emptiness, stillness, tranquility . . . silence, non-action—this is the level of heaven and earth. This is perfect Tao. Wise men find here their resting place. Resting, they are empty.*

Waiting means stillness of mind in whatever the activity. If we are always busy trying to help the Dharma along, it prevents us from seeing clearly, from receiving the strength and understanding that comes out of silence, from stopping the internal dialogue. For as long as the internal dialogue goes on, so long do we remain in a prison of words which keeps us from relating in an open and spontaneous way to the world—a world that's very different from what our preconceptions lead us to imagine. Stopping the internal dialogue is the ability to wait and to listen.

It was listening to the voice of his heart which led Siddhartha from his father to the ascetics, and then from the forest into a worldly life of business and love. But slowly that quality of listening became jaded by over-indulgence in sense pleasures. He became so involved in his desires that he no longer could hear. Full of despair he dragged himself to the side of a river, and was about to drown himself when he heard from the river, from his heart, the sound of "Aum." And staying there by the river for many years he again learned to listen, to wait.

Siddhartha listened. He was now listening intently, completely absorbed, quite empty. Taking in everything. He felt that he had now completely learned the art of listening. He had often heard all this before, all these numerous voices in the river. But today they sounded different. He could no longer distinguish the different voices, the merry voice from the weeping one, the childish from the manly one. They all belonged to each other. The lament of those who yearn, the laughter of the wise, the cry of the indignant, and the groan of dying. They were all interwoven and interlocked, entwined in a thousand ways. All the voices, all the goals, all the yearnings, the sorrows, the pleasures, all the good and evil, all of them together with the world, all of them together with the stream of events and the music of life. When Siddhartha listened attentively to this river, to this song of a thousand voices, when he did not listen to the sorrow or laughter, did not bind himself to any one particular voice and absorb it into himself, but heard them all, the unity—then the great song of a thousand voices consisted of one word—perfection.

The third power of Siddhartha was fasting. Fasting means giving up, renunciation, surrender. It means energy and effort and strength. Power and lightness of mind come from renunciation. Often people think that giving things up, or fasting, is a burden and source of suffering, not realizing the joy and simplicity in being unencumbered by unnecessary possessions and incessant desires. There is no super-human effort needed to practice renunciation; the energy required is only to overcome our inertia and old habit patterns. When this effort is put forth we experience a spaciousness and ease of mind which comes from the letting go of attachments.

Fasting means simplicity. One of the joys of studying in India, even though there were many difficulties in health and food and living arrangements, was the basic simplicity of life. It was not encumbered by many of the things that burden us in America. Travelers passing through would wonder how we could "renounce" so many things—electricity and hot running water, not understanding the lightness of living so simply. From simplicity of living, from not needing to have or possess so much, come contentment and peace.

Fasting, renunciation. We can experiment with this letting go in our lives through generosity, through establishing ourselves in basic moral restraint, through practicing giving up the things which bind us. Renunciation happens on all levels, not only in our relationships to material objects or people. There is a Taoist phrase "fasting of the heart" which describes the perfection of inner renunciation. Chuang Tzu wrote,

The goal of fasting is inner unity. This means hearing, but not with the ear; hearing, but not with the understanding; hearing with the spirit, with your whole being. The hearing that is only in the ears is one thing. The hearing of the understanding is another. But the hearing of the spirit is not limited to any one faculty, to the ear, or to the mind. Hence it demands the emptiness of all the faculties. And when the faculties are empty, then the whole being listens. There is then a direct grasp of what is right there before you that can never be heard with the ear or understood with the mind. Fasting of the heart empties the faculties, frees you from limitation and from preoccupation. Fasting of the heart begets unity and freedom.

Siddhartha could think. He could wait. He could fast. These are the qualities of a warrior which are developed in coming to understanding the totality of oneself. When you sit, when you walk, when you are impeccably aware all day long, these are the qualities which are being awakened.

Question: *Don Juan speaks of personal power. How does this relate to practice?*

Answer: Strength of mind is power. Not the power which extends itself to manipulate, but the power of penetrating insight, the power to understand. Don Juan said that even if one were told the deepest secrets of the universe, they would appear as just empty words until there was enough personal power. What this power means is strength, steadiness, the ability to penetrate deeply into how things are happening. It develops as the mind becomes more concentrated. From penetrating power comes insight; with strength of mind a single word is enough to open new levels of understanding. In a meditation retreat it is the continuity of practice which develops this kind of personal power.

Are there any clear signs along the way that distinguish intuition and insight from imagination?

Intuitions come out of the silent mind; imagination is conceptual. There's a vast difference. That's why the development of insight does not come from thinking about things, it comes from the development of a silence of mind in which a clear vision, a clear seeing, can happen. The whole progress of insight, the whole development of understanding, comes at times when the mind is quiet. Then a sudden, "Aha, that's how things are!" In the Zen teachings of Huang Po, it talks about insight as being a sudden, wordless understanding. That kind of intuition has a certainty about it because it's not the product of some thought or image but rather a sudden clear perception of how things are.

In practice, how is using the mind to probe and investigate related to choiceless awareness?

Many ways of developing insight use a directed awareness. We can direct the attention toward various aspects of the process, such as posture, or bodily sensations, or thoughts, as a way of probing specific areas. But even a directed awareness, once it is settled on an area, is really choiceless. Then it's sitting back and watching what's happening, without judging, without clinging or condemning. Sometimes people are very timid in their practice, always looking for the rules of how to do it, afraid to make a mistake. Insight comes from mindfulness, and either we're aware of what's happening or not. There's no way of being mindful wrong. Exercise the mind, exercise this probing quality. Be deeply watchful of how thoughts arise out of nothing and pass away into nothing. Or probe into a pain, get on the inside of it. Exercise the mind in a fearless way, not thinking about things, but with silent awareness. The mind can become very malleable. If you work a piece of clay in making pottery, it becomes soft and easily shaped. When the awareness and concentration are developed, the mind also has that kind of workability and flexibility. Explore all aspects of the mind-body process. When I was in India, I lived on the second floor of an ashram. I used to go up and down the steps many times a day, each time exploring the mechanism of climbing a step, how the knee has to work, how the weight shifts. It's an interesting process. In all of the activities there should be that kind of interest. Seeing, exploring how things are happening. And at other times it's just sitting back and doing nothing, a choiceless awareness, watching the natural unfolding.

How did this whole process of mind and body all begin?

There's a story of a man who was shot by a poison arrow. His friends came with a doctor and wanted to remove the arrow and treat the wound. But the man said, "No, you can't take it out, I have to know who shot the arrow and where he came from and from what kind of a tree the shaft for the arrow was made and what kind of bird feathers are at the end of the arrow." Certainly that man would die before he could get an answer to all those questions. In the same way, the Buddha said that a lot of philosophical speculation about the origin of the world, the origin of the universe, about how it all started, is like that man who's been shot with the poison arrow. We find ourselves in a certain predicament; the predicament is one of being a mind-body that is often full of anger and greed, ignorance and pain. The task is to take the arrow out, to free the mind from those qualities, to free ourselves from suffering. The questions which are most relevant are those which apply to what we are experiencing right now.

Why does greed arise?

When we see something pleasant, we want to hold on, not understanding the impermanence of it all. As soon as we become mindful, paying attention to what's happening, seeing how everything is arising and passing away, the grasping and greed decreases. There's nothing to hold onto. It's all bubbles. And the experience of impermanence, the dissolving of the solidity of everything, brings about the letting go, the state of non-attachment. It all comes about through being aware, through being impeccable.

It's inspiring to become a warrior. There's no one else who can do it for us. We each have to do it for ourselves. Be aware, moment to moment, paying attention to what's happening in a total way. There's nothing mystical about it, it's so simple and direct and straightforward; but it takes doing. That's what the meditation is all about.

•

Concentration Game

Today we're going to play a game. It's called the concentration game. The rules are these: In the next hour, for every breath that you exhale, count one. The next breath, two; up to ten. Not missing a breath. For each out breath, or falling of the abdomen, count one number. If you miss the count because you forget what number you're on—back to one. If you miss a count because your mind wanders and goes off the breath—back to one. Ignore everything else.

There are some things which may begin to happen. The breath may become erratic, fast or slow, fine or deep. Stay with it. One to ten. Then begin one to ten again. It may be that after about five minutes, the mind starts thinking, "This is stupid, I'm not going to sit here for an hour and count to ten." Keep counting. And if, because of that thought you miss a breath, back to one again. It may be that all kinds of pains and tensions arise in the body. Ignore them. One to ten. This is a way to specifically strengthen the one-pointedness factor of mind, training it to stay on a single object. If you find the game useful in your practice, from time to time you can incorporate it in your sittings.

•

Three Pillars of Dharma: Parami

To practice and understand the Dharma is a rare and precious thing. Few people in the world are presented with this opportunity. Most people are circling around, driven by ignorance and desire, unaware of the possibility of getting off this wheel of samsara, the wheel of greed and hatred. Opportunities to practice arise because of something which in the Pali language is called "parami." Parami means the accumulated force of purity within the mind. Every mind-moment that is free of greed, hatred and delusion has a certain purifying force in the flow of consciousness; and in our long evolution, we have accumulated many of these forces of purity within our minds.

Sometimes in English this word parami is loosely translated as merit. But that is easily misunderstood as collecting gold stars for good deeds. Rather, parami is the force of purity within the mind. When there is a great accumulation of the factors of non-greed, non-hatred, non-delusion, the paramis become forceful and result in all kinds of happiness, from the most worldly sensual pleasures to the highest happiness of enlightenment. Nothing is happening as an accident, or without cause.

There are two kinds of parami: purity of conduct and purity of wisdom. The forces of purification involved in right conduct become the cause of happy surroundings, pleasant circumstances, agreeable relationships, and the opportunity to hear the Dharma. For example, the situation of this retreat did not happen by chance. It happened because there were strong forces of purity within each of us.

The other kind of parami, purity of wisdom, develops by practicing right understanding, and it makes possible the growth of insight. Both kinds of paramis, both these forces of purification, have to be developed in order for us to have the chance to practice the Dharma, and then the wisdom to understand.

There are three pillars of Dharma, three fields of action, which cultivate and strengthen the paramis. The first of these is generosity. Giving is the expression in action of the mental factor of non-greed. Non-greed means letting go, not holding on, not grasping, not clinging. Every time we share something, or give something away, it strengthens this wholesome factor, until it becomes a powerful force in the mind. The Buddha said that if we knew, as he did, the fruit of giving, we would not let a single meal pass without sharing.

The karmic results of generosity are abundance and deep harmonious relationships with other people. Sharing what we have is a beautiful way of relating to others, and our friendships are much enhanced by the quality of generosity. Even more significantly, the cultivation of non-greed becomes a strong force for liberation. What keeps us bound is desire and grasping in our own minds. As we practice giving we learn to let go.

It is said that there are three kinds of givers. The first are beggarly givers. They give only after much hesitation, and then just the leftovers, the worst of what they have. They think, "Should I give or shouldn't I? Maybe it's too much?" And finally perhaps part with something they don't really want.

74

Friendly givers are people who give what they themselves would use. They share what they have and with less deliberation, with more open-handedness.

The highest kind of givers are kingly givers who offer the very best of what they have. They share spontaneously and in the moment without needing to deliberate. Giving has become natural to their conduct. Non-greed is so strong in their minds that at every opportunity they share what is treasured most in an easy and loving way.

For some people giving is difficult; the greed factor is strong and there is a lot of attachment. For others generosity comes easily. It doesn't matter. From wherever we're starting, we simply begin to practice. Every act of generosity slowly weakens the factor of greed. Sharing openly is a beautiful way to live in the world, and through practice we can all become kingly givers.

There are two kinds of consciousness which are involved in our actions. One is called "prompted consciousness": the mind which considers and deliberates before acting. The other is called "unprompted," and is very spontaneous. When a particular action has been cultivated, there is no longer the need to deliberate. Just in the moment, very spontaneously, this unprompted consciousness operates. Through practice, we develop the kind of consciousness where giving becomes the natural expression of mind.

In one of the Buddha's previous lives (when he was called a "bodhisattva," meaning a being working towards enlightenment), he came to the top of a cliff and saw a tigress with two young cubs. The tigress was ill and had no milk to feed her cubs. Out of compassion for the tigress and her cubs, without regard for or identification with his own body, he threw himself off the cliff to be food for the tigress so she would be strong enough to give milk. A very kingly gift.

We may not reach that height of selflessness, but the story points the direction: to cultivate generosity out of compassion and love for all other beings. In many discourses, the Buddha urged people to practice giving until it becomes an effortless expression of understanding. Generosity is a great parami; it is listed as the first of the perfections of the Buddha. And as it is cultivated it becomes the cause of great happiness in our lives.

The second pillar of the Dharma, or field of purifying action, is moral restraint. For people in the world, for householders, this means following the five basic precepts: not killing, not stealing, not commiting sexual misconduct, not using wrong speech, and not taking intoxicants which cloud the mind and make it dull.

All beings want to live and be happy; all beings want to be free of pain. It is a much lighter state of mind to preserve life than to destroy it. It feels so much better to gently remove an insect from inside our home and put it outside than to kill it. Having a reverence for all living things.

Not stealing means refraining from taking those things which are not given to us.

Sexual misconduct can be most easily understood as refraining from those actions of sensuality which cause pain and harm to others, or turbulence or disturbance in ourselves.

Refraining from wrong speech means not only telling the truth, but avoiding a lot of useless and frivolous talk. A lot of our time is spent in gossip. Things come to mind and we talk without considering their usefulness. Restraint of speech is very helpful in making the mind peaceful. Not using harsh or abusive language. Our speech should be gentle, cultivating harmony and unity between people.

When walking on the path of enlightenment, toward freedom and clarity of mind, it is also not very helpful to take things which cloud the mind and make it dull. Often, too, carelessness which results from intoxication weakens our resolve to keep the other precepts.

The importance and value of the precepts is on many levels. They act as a protection for us, a guard against the creation of unwholesome karma. All of these acts from which we refrain involve motives of either greed, hatred or delusion, and are karmically productive of future pain and suffering. While mindfulness is still being developed and at times not yet very strong, the resolution to follow the precepts will serve as a reminder if we are about to commit some unskillful act. For example, you're about to kill a mosquito, your hand is ready to swat it, and just at that moment the force of the precept to refrain from killing will become operative and be the cause of greater awareness.

Unskillful actions also cause in the moment of doing them a heaviness and darkness in the mind. Every skillful action, every restraint from unwholesome activity, causes lightness and clarity. As you carefully observe the mind engaged in various activities you will begin to experience that any activity based on greed, hatred and delusion causes a heaviness to arise. Following these moral precepts as a rule for living keeps us light, and allows the mind to be open and clear. It is a much easier and less complicated way to live. At this level of understanding, the precepts are not taken as commandments but are followed for the effect they have on our quality of life. There is no sense of imposition at all because they are the natural expression of a clear mind.

The precepts have an even more profound meaning on the spiritual path. They free the mind of remorse and anxiety. Guilt about past actions is not very helpful, and keeps the mind agitated. By establishing basic purity of action in the present the mind more easily becomes tranquil and one-pointed. Without concentration, insight is impossible. And so the foundation in morality becomes the basis of spiritual development.

The third field of purifying activity is meditation. Meditation is divided into two main streams. The first is the development of concentration, the ability of the mind to stay steady on an object, without wavering and wandering. When the mind is concentrated, there is a great power of penetration. The mind that is scattered cannot see into the nature of the mind and body. A certain degree of one-pointedness is essential to the growth of wisdom. But concentration by itself is not enough. That strong force in the mind has to be employed in the service of understanding, which is the second kind of meditation: the cultivation of insight. That means seeing clearly the process of things, the nature of all dharmas. Everything is impermanent and in flow, arising and passing away moment to moment. Consciousness, the object, all the different mental factors, the body: all phenomena share in the flow of impermanence. When the mind is clear it experiences this ceaseless change on a microscopic level: instant to instant we are being born and dying. There is nothing to hold onto, nothing to grasp at. No state of mind or body, no situation outside ourselves is to be grasped at, because it is all changing in the moment. The development of insight means experiencing the flow of impermanence within ourselves so that we begin to let go, not grasping so desperately at mind-body phenomena.

Experiencing impermanence leads to an understanding of the inherent unsatisfactoriness of the mind-body process: unsatisfactory in the sense that it is incapable of giving any lasting happiness. If we think that the body is going to be the cause of our permanent peace and happiness and joy, then we're not seeing the inevitable decay that's going to occur. As we begin to get old and diseased and decay and die, people with a strong attachment to the body will experience great suffering. Inherent in all things which arise is decay. All the elements of matter, all the elements of mind, are arising and vanishing.

The third characteristic of all existence which is seen very clearly with the development of insight and awareness is that in all this flow of phenomena there is no such thing as an "I," or "self," a "me," or "mine." It is all impersonal phenomena flowing on, empty phenomena, empty of self. There is no entity behind it all who is experiencing it. The experiencer, the knower, is itself part of the process. As insight is cultivated through the practice of mindfulness, these three characteristics of existence are revealed.

Suppose you have a pond of water which is filled with weeds. Practicing moral restraint is like going down to the water and pushing the weeds aside to get a handful to drink. The weeds are still present, and when you take your hand away, once again they come back and cover the pond. In moments of moral behavior the mind is pure, but as soon as we are forgetful, the defilements are there again. If you build a fence in the pond which keeps all the weeds on the outside, the water within remains clear to drink for as long as the fence is there. But the weeds are still on the outside and if the fence is removed the weeds come back. That's like the force of concentration in the mind. It suppresses all the defilements. Insight or wisdom is like going down to the pond and pulling out the weeds: you pull one out and then another until the whole pond is clear. When removed in that way, they do not come back. Insight is a purification process: when all the negativities in our mind have been looked at, examined, and finally uprooted, they do not arise again.

Wisdom is the culmination of the spiritual path, which starts with the practice of generosity, moral restraint, and the development of concentration. From that base of purity comes penetrating insight into the nature of the mind and body. By being perfectly aware in the moment, all that has been accumulated in our minds begins to surface. All the thoughts and emotions, all the ill will and greed and desire, all the lust, all the love, all the energy, all the confidence and joy, everything that is within our minds begins to be brought to the conscious level. And through the practice of mindfulness, of not clinging, not condemning, not identifying with anything, the mind becomes lighter and freer.

An indication of the relative power of these various fields of parami was given by the Buddha. He said that the power of purification in giving is augmented by the purity of the receiver. But many times more powerful even than having made an offering to the Buddha himself or the entire order of enlightened monks and

79

nuns is to practice the thought of lovingkindness with a concentrated mind. And yet more potent than cultivating that loving thought is clearly seeing the impermanence of all phenomena, because it is this insight into impermanence which is the beginning of freedom.

Question: *For a while I found myself giving too much away; I got very strung out on giving. Could you talk about the nature of giving when it leads to feeling strung out?*

Answer: We all are at different levels. We're not all at the level of the bodhisattva who gave his life to feed the tiger and her cubs. There might be a momentary impulse to do something like that followed by many moments of regret. That is not skillful. We have to be sensitive to where we are in the present moment and cultivate generosity which feels appropriate. It grows. As we practice giving it becomes increasingly spontaneous. And when it develops with that balance, then it's harmonious, and there is no regret which follows.

The precepts can be a guide for a certain level but is there a danger of clinging to them? Can't they become a hindrance because they are concepts? There may be actions arising out of compassion which will be against the precepts like lying to spare somebody. What happens when the precepts and intuition conflict?

All these fields of purifying activity are very much to be understood in terms of the mental factors they're cultivating, not the action itself. If we do an action out of compassion, then it's wholesome. But often we're not at that place of awareness where we can perceive all the factors involved in every activity. Until we reach the level of sensitivity where we're really tuned into every motivating aspect of our actions, where we can determine whether it's skillful or unskillful, these precepts serve as a very useful guideline. A monk once came to the Buddha and said he couldn't remember the more than 200 rules necessary for the monks, much less follow them. The Buddha said, "Can you remember one rule?" And the monk said he thought he could. The Buddha said, "Be mindful." Everything else comes out of that awareness. If you're very mindful, automatically there's right action.

I see a conflict between being a kingly giver and being secure in the world.

The cultivation of kingly giving does not necessarily mean that we go out and give everything away. It means giving with a great openness, appropriate to the situation. We have a certain responsibility to ourselves to keep things together so we can continue the practice and cultivate the factors of enlightenment. The level of giving will very much depend upon the particular evolution of mind. There should not be an image of how one should be giving, and then trying to live up to that image. Simply, in the present moment, take opportunities to cultivate the factor of non-greed. It's not complicated, let it unfold by itself. When it gets to the point where you're ready to fling yourself over a cliff to feed the tigers, you will.

I'm a little confused about not lying. When you don't verbalize something that you're thinking that seems truthful and appropriate to the situation, is that considered lying?

There could be something true, a true perception, which would not be of help to another person perhaps because they were not in a place where they could hear it. We should speak the truth when it is useful. It's beautiful and peaceful to stay in a place of silence of mind. But that takes a lot of mindfulness because we're very conditioned to a lot of talk. The words come out before we are even aware that there was an intention to do so. It's all very mechanical. But as the mindfulness gets sharper, we begin to be aware before talking—the intention to speak arises and we're mindful of it. Then we can begin to see both whether it's truthful and also useful.

•

St. John of the Cross/ St. Francis de Sales

In the writings of some Christian mystics there are teachings very relevant to our practice. From St. John of the Cross:

> *It is not from want of will that I have refrained from writing to you, for truly do I wish you all good; but because it seemed to me that enough had been said already to effect all that is needful, and that what is wanting (if indeed anything be wanting) is not writing or speaking—whereof ordinarily there is more than enough—but silence and work. Where speaking distracts, silence and work collect the thoughts and strengthen the spirit. As soon therefore as a person understands what has been said to him for his good, there is no further need to hear or to discuss; but to set himself in earnest to practice what he has learnt with silence and attention. . .*

It's not an easy thing that we have set about to do, this training and purification of the mind. It requires a great deal of patience and perseverance. It does not happen by itself. But with gentle persistence it is possible.

St. Francis de Sales wrote:

If the heart wanders or is distracted, bring it back to the point quite gently. . . And even if you did nothing during the whole of your hour but bring your heart back, though it went away every time you brought it back, your hour would be very well employed.

Do not be discouraged by wandering thoughts or daydreams. Each time there is awareness of the mind wandering, gently bring it back to the breath or sensations. No matter how many times this happens, if each time the wandering mind is brought back, the hour will be well spent. Be gentle with yourself. Be persevering. Though it may not be apparent to you, there is a great transformation taking place. It is like fruit ripening on a tree. As the sun shines on it, the fruit ripens, although from one day to the next, the process may be imperceptible. In the same way, the changes and ripening in our own mind are also going on. And as St. John of the Cross said, it is in silence and work that this transformation is brought to completion.

•

Four Noble Truths

There is so much suffering in the world. Every day there are millions of people who do not have enough to eat, suffering the pains of hunger. There are millions of people in the world who don't have enough clothes or shelter, experiencing the pain of cold, rain, and heat. There are so many millions who are suffering the pain of disease, even when the remedy is known, because they are unable to get any kind of treatment. There is the suffering of birth. The pain of the mother. Even more pain for the child being born, forced through a narrow opening, feeling the abrasive elements of the external world. The body gets diseased, it gets sick, it gets old and decrepit. The pain of death.

There are so many beings in the world helpless in the hands of enemies, in the hands of people who want to do them harm. In so many countries prisoners are right now being brutalized. There is the violence of war. Men and women with feelings just like our own, helpless in the face of pain, unable to do anything about it. How many times have we been in that very same situation, and how many times will we be there in future wanderings. One little turn of the karmic wheel and we again are those people. In having this physical body of ours, there is such potential for suffering. How many times have we experienced it, and how often will we continue to do so?

The material elements of our bodies are called the four great primary elements. They're called great because of their destructive power. These same four elements which constitute our body are those which constitute the earth and the sun, the planets and stars. It is these very elements, experienced in the body, which in following their natural laws are responsible for the creation and destruction of whole solar systems and galaxies. The power of these elements is enormous. For a very short period of time the elements are in some kind of balance. So we forget, not realizing the tremendous destructive power inherent in them, until, following their own nature, they begin to get out of balance and cause decay, the dissolution of the body, great pain and death.

We are like children playing in a house being consumed by fire. Children playing with toys, taking delight in momentary pleasures, completely unaware of the fire raging all around. But heaven is kind because it sends messengers to tell of the danger, to point out the pain and suffering which is on all sides:

Did you never see in the world a man or a woman 80, 90, or 100 years old, frail, crooked as a gabled roof, bent down, resting on crutches, tottering steps, infirm, youth long since fled, with broken teeth, gray and scanty hair, or none, and does the thought never come to you that you, too, are subject to decay? That you, too, cannot escape it?

Did you never see in the world a man or a woman sick, afflicted and grievously ill, wallowing in his own filth, lifted up by some, put to bed by others, and did the thought never come to you that you, too, are subject to sickness? That you, too, cannot escape it?

Did you never see in the world the corpse of a man, one, two, or three days after death, swollen up, blue-black in color, and full of corruption and did the thought never come to you that you, too, are subject to death? That you, too, cannot escape it?

86

We, too, are subject to exactly these same things. Death is not for some while sparing others. It is the end for us all. There is no escape from this fact.

There is the pain of mind. Depression. Despair. Anxiety. Worry. Anger. Hatred. Fear. Lust. Grief. How long will we remain ensnared in this long round of rebirths, hurrying on, driven by ignorance and craving? The pain of this endlessness, every morning to awaken to colors and smells, sounds and sensations, thoughts, in endless repetition. We go through the day, and to sleep, and we wake to the same colors and sounds and smells and tastes and sensations and thoughts, over and over again.

> *Inconceivable is the beginning of this samsara. Not to be discovered is the first beginning of beings who, obstructed by ignorance and ensnared by craving, are hurrying and hastening through this round of rebirths. Which do you think is more, the flood of tears which, weeping and wailing, you have shed upon this long way, hurrying and hastening through this round of rebirths, united with the undesired, separated from the desired, this—or the waters of the four great oceans? Long have you suffered the deaths of fathers and mothers and sons and daughters, brothers and sisters, and while you were thus suffering, you have shed more tears upon this long way than there is water in the four great oceans. And, thus, have you long undergone suffering, undergone torment, undergone misfortune, and filled the graveyards full. Long enough to be dissatisfied with all forms of existence, long enough to turn away and to free yourselves from them all.*

Like children playing with toys in a burning house, we do not like to look at the pain and suffering in our lives. We put the old and sick away in homes so we don't have to see their sorrow. We chase beggars off the street so we don't see the affliction of poverty. We dress up corpses as if they were going to a party, never confronting the face of death. The first noble truth of the Buddha's enlightenment is the truth of suffering. It does no good to pretend that it does not exist. No matter how we obscure it, the body is going to get old and diseased. It is going to die. No matter how many distractions we are entertained with, there will be anger and ill will and frustration and anxiety and tension. We burn with anger, burn with desire. The first noble truth, the truth of suffering.

The Buddha did not stop there. He pointed out the truth of suffering and also explained the causes. What is it that binds us to this wheel of sorrow? The Buddha saw that the bondage is in our own minds, it is the bondage of attachment. We are on this wheel of pain because we cling to it, and we cling to it out of ignorance.

There are four great attachments which keep us bound to the wheel. The first of these is our attachment to sense pleasures. Always seeking pleasant sounds and sights, agreeable smells, delicious tastes, and pleasant sensations of the body. The endless seeking of momentary, fragmentary pleasures. We are attracted to them as if they will solve our problems, as if they will bring an end to suffering. We live our lives waiting for the next two-week vacation, the next relationship, some new object to "own": waiting with desire for some new happiness always just out of reach.

There is a story about the Mulla Nazruddin, a famous Sufi teaching figure. One day he went to the market place and saw a big bushel of hot chili peppers on sale. He bought them, returned home, and began to eat. A little while later his disciples came and saw the Mulla with tears streaming down his face, his mouth and tongue burning. "Mulla, Mulla, why do you go on eating them?" As he reached for another, Nazruddin replied, "I keep waiting for a sweet one."

The second great attachment is to our own opinions and views. We have so many opinions about things, so many preconceptions. Attachment to view is such a great bondage. It keeps us from seeing how things are; it filters reality through the colored glasses of our own particular conditioning. A great meditation master from Thailand when asked what was the greatest hindrance his students had, answered, "Opinions, views and ideas about all things. About

88

themselves, about practice, about the teachings of the Buddha. Their minds are filled with opinions about things. They are too clever to listen to others. It is like water in a cup. If the cup is filled with dirty, stale water, it is useless. Only after the old water is thrown out can the cup become useful. You must empty your minds of opinions, then you will see."

In the Sutra of the Third Zen Patriarch, it says, "Do not seek the truth. Only cease to cherish opinions." If we let go of this attachment, the whole Dharma will be revealed. Everything will be there. We have to let go of our preconceived ideas of how things are, of how we would like things to be. Letting go of the attachment to our cherished opinions. This is the second of the great bonds which keeps us going around on the wheel of samsara, the wheel of suffering.

The third kind of attachment is to different rites and rituals: thinking that if a stick of incense is lit or a candle placed on an altar everything will be fine. All the practices people do, all the ceremonies, in the hope that lighting a candle or a stick of incense or saying some kind of prayer or mantra will bring this suffering to an end. Even attachment to practice, becoming spiritually self-righteous, or any kind of spiritual materialism is a fetter. These attachments are a great bondage.

The fourth of the bonds and the most subtle, the most deeply conditioned, is our attachment to the belief in self, in I, in me, in mine. The belief that there is some permanent entity in the mind-body which is experiencing all of this. Because of this belief, and to satisfy the I, the self, we get involved in all kinds of unwholesome actions, all kinds of greed and hatred, all kinds of delusion, for the gratification of the self, which isn't even there. Our attachment to the concept of self is so great that everything we do revolves about it, tying the bonds even tighter to this mass of pain.

The second noble truth of the Buddha's enlightenment is the cause of suffering: desire and attachment. Desire for sense pleasure, cherishing views and opinions, the belief that rites, rituals and ceremonies are going to bring a relief to suffering, and the very strong attachment we have to the concept of self, of I. No one makes us hold on. There is no force or power outside of ourselves which keeps us bound to the wheel of life and death. It is just the clinging in our own minds.

There is a kind of monkey trap used in Asia. A coconut is hollowed out and attached by a rope to a tree or stake in the ground. At the bottom of the coconut a small slit is made and some sweet food is placed inside. The hole on the bottom is just big enough for the monkey to slide in his open hand, but does not allow for a closed fist to pass out. The monkey smells the sweets, reaches in with his hand to grasp the food and is then unable to withdraw it. The clenched fist won't pass through the opening. When the hunters come, the monkey becomes frantic but cannot get away. There is no one keeping that monkey captive, except the force of his own attachment. All that he has to do is open his hand. But so strong is the force of greed in the mind that it is a rare monkey which can let go. It is the desires and clinging in our own minds which keep us trapped. All we need do is open our hands, let go of our selves, our attachments, and be free.

The third noble truth of the Buddha's enlightenment is the end of suffering, the end of pain. Nirvana is the state beyond the mind-body process, not subject to all the suffering which is inherent in it. Freedom. Peace. Calm. Cool. Release. A putting down of the burden.

Nirvana is of two kinds. The first is momentary nirvana, freedom from defilement, freedom from greed, hatred and delusion, a putting out of these fires in the mind moment to moment. Every moment of freedom from defilements is a moment of coolness and peace. The other meaning of nirvana is the state beyond the process altogether, the ending of the burden of suffering, the quenching of the fire.

An example is given of beings who live in a very barren desert. There is little water, not enough food, and no protection from the blazing sun. Because that's all those people know, they take it to be a satisfactory place to live. But then one of them travels to a land where there is coolness and abundance, where there is water, food and shelter, and he realizes the impoverished conditions, the suffering of the place in which he formerly lived. In comparison to the peace and stillness and silence of nirvana, the endless mind-body process, the endless arising and passing away is such a great burden, such a great suffering. The third noble truth is the experience indicated by the Buddha when he said that there is no higher happiness than peace.

The Buddha also pointed out the way to this experience. It is not a mysterious teaching reserved for just a few. The fourth noble truth of the Buddha's teachings is the noble eightfold path, how to put down the burden.

It is not an extreme path. It does not involve great self torture. It does not involve going off to a cave. It is neither self-mortification, nor over-indulgence in the sense pleasures which keep us bound. It is the middle path. To be aware. Aware of how things are happening. To be wakeful and balanced. To be mindful. Not clinging. Not condemning. Not identifying with things as being I or self. Moment to moment freeing the mind from defilements.

The truth of suffering is to be realized. The truth of the cause of suffering is to be understood. The truth of the end of suffering is to be experienced. And the way to the end is to be walked by each one. The Buddha's enlightenment solved his problem, it did not solve ours, except to point out the way. There is no magic formula which will release us from suffering. Each of us has to purify our own mind, for it is the attachment in our minds that keeps us bound.

FIFTEENTH
AFTERNOON

•

Halfway Resolution

In the sitting practice, stillness of body is a great help in achieving stillness of mind. As a way of making the concentration strong, at the beginning of some sittings, make a resolution not to change position for that hour. The first few times might be difficult, but if the resolution is impeccable, you can sit and observe whatever comes. Even if you find the mind getting restless or reactive or tense or filled with aversion towards pain, there's value in making the resolution and fulfilling it. Both the concentration and effort factors are greatly strengthened, and after the first few hour sittings you will find that it becomes easier to stay still.

Keep the mind in a place of non-resistance to any object at all. Then nothing becomes an obstacle or hindrance. All objects of mind or body, internal or external, pass by, in the clear field of awareness. Make no movement of the mind toward or away from any object: non-doing of mind. Then there will be a perfect stillness and balance in which one sees clearly, in the moment, the arising and passing away of the breath, of sensations, of thoughts, of emotions, of sounds, of smells, of images.

Be aware of the flow of impermanence. There is nothing to hold on to, nothing to grasp at. There is a paragraph at the end of *Mount Analogue* which illustrates the force of this flow and the appropriate stance to take:

> *Never halt on a shifting slope. Even if you think you have a firm foothold, as you take time to catch your breath and look at the sky, the ground will settle little by little under your weight. The gravel will begin to slip imperceptibly and suddenly it will drop away under you and launch you like a ship. The mountain is always watching for a chance to give you a spill.*

There is no time to stop, even for a moment, to try to hold on. With every moment of trying to cling, we get caught up, carried away by our thoughts, projections and concepts.

The retreat is now about halfway over; often in the middle of retreats, however long they are, the mind goes through a doldrum. It gets a little lazy and lax and restless. The mind starts thinking it has made a big effort all this time, and now it can relax its efforts.

Be mindful of this. Now is the time to arouse energy, not to slacken. Think of how very much you have done in the first two weeks. Think back to when you first started and how difficult it was to sit still for just an hour. A great strength of mind has been developing, a momentum of concentration and mindfulness. The beginning of the retreat was laying the foundation, overcoming the gross kind of hindrances, the kind that prevent us from sitting still even for an hour. Those initial difficulties have been more or less successfully dealt with. The mind has settled down. It has begun to penetrate, begun to see how the mind-body process is working. Insight is maturing. It is difficult to see it in ourselves because the changes are happening almost imperceptibly moment to moment. But the practice is slowly deepening. Even more can yet be done in the remaining time. It takes a great stirring up of energy not to let the mind sink into a lull.

Renew the effort to maintain silence. Silence is an energy giver. It creates a clarity in which all the aspects of the mind are clearly seen. If every time restlessness or sloth or laziness arises we begin talking, the opportunity is missed to see through it. Silence enables us to be attentive to what is going on, to all the ups and downs. The purpose of meditation is not to sit back in a state of bliss for a month. It is to experience the totality of the mind and body. To experience fully all the pains and aches, all the blissful sensations, all the times of sharp focus, all the restlessness and boredom. Silence provides the space of solitude in which all of this can be clearly seen. A lot of talking creates a spiraling downward. We become restless; we start talking; then it becomes even more difficult to concentrate and the mind becomes yet more restless. Making effort, rousing energy and creating solitude around yourself will intensify the practice. No one can be sure when the opportunity for practice will come again. There are very special circumstances for us in this environment. It is the perfect place to explore ourselves, to find out who we are. Don't waste the opportunity.

Another great help in rousing mindfulness is slowing down. Slow down your actions. Make every movement of the body all day long an object of meditation. From the moment of getting up to the moment of going to sleep, notice everything very clearly, very sharply: every movement in bathing, in dressing, in eating. Our habitual way of doing things is to rush, toppling forward into the next moment or the next activity, being always in transition. Make an effort to settle back into the moment. There's no hurry. There is no place to go. The whole purpose of being here is to cultivate the ability to notice what's happening in the moment. Don't force or strain. Settle back without planning or anticipating. Keep a relaxed but sharply attentive mind. The mind will penetrate to deeper and deeper levels. Keeping silence and slowing down helps not only ourselves but everyone around us. When we see someone else speeding along, it awakens that in us. In seeing someone else be mindful, we ourselves become more awake. Be aware of the value and help you are to others. The retreat is a beautiful balance; working on ourselves in silence and solitude, yet being in the supportive atmosphere of a group.

SIXTEENTH
EVENING

•

Karma

The Buddha was once asked why some people are born rich, others poor; why some people have healthy bodies, others sickly. Why is it that some people are very beautiful and others ugly? Why some have many friends and others none? What accounted for all the differences that can be seen among people? He replied that all beings are the inheritors, the heirs, of their own past karma. It is really our past deeds which are the womb out of which we are born. Life as it is experienced in the present is the result of the accumulated force of all past actions.

The Buddha went on to explain what kinds of actions produced which particular results. He said that beings who take the life of others live just a short time. Beings who refrain from killing, experience a long life-span. People who cause harm, cause pain to other living things, experience a lot of disease and sickness. Those who practice harmlessness towards others, non-violence, experience good health. He said those who are greedy, miserly, experience great poverty. Those beings who practice generosity, sharing, open-handedness, experience abundance. This is the law of cause and effect at work. Each action produces a certain result.

People who indulge in a lot of harsh, abusive language, in angry words, take on an ugly appearance. Those who practice loving, gentle, harmonious speech, experience great beauty as the result. We are all the inheritors of our past deeds. Those beings who engage in disharmonious behavior, such as adultery or stealing, have the result of being associated with unwise people, do not have many good friends, do not come into contact with the Dharma. Those who practice the basic moral restraints will live in pleasant surroundings, have many good friends and many helps along the path. Those who never question what this life is all about, who never investigate their minds, who never try to analyze or understand the nature of things, are born dull and stupid. Those people who question, who probe, who investigate, who try to seek out the answers to this mystery of life become very wise. Again, it is the law of cause and effect at work.

There is no one up in the sky who destines us to a particular role, to a particular kind of life. Understanding how the law of karma works enables us to begin shaping our own destiny. There is a path leading to all the high and happy states and one that leads to suffering. When we understand the paths we are free to choose which we will follow.

There are four main groups of karma which operate in our lives. The first is called reproductive karma. It is the force of those actions we do which have the power to determine rebirth. The kind of actions we do which determine whether we are born in the human world or lower worlds, the heaven or Brahmic planes of existence.

The next kind of karma is called supportive karma. It is those actions which support the reproductive karma. For example, suppose we have good reproductive karma and take birth in the human world. That is a good rebirth, a happy plane of existence. Supportive karma are all those deeds which make our experience as a human being pleasant. It reinforces good reproductive karma, and is the cause of all kinds of happiness.

The third group is called counter-active karma. It obstructs the reproductive karma. Suppose we have the good karma of rebirth as a human being, but we experience a lot of trouble, a lot of pain, a lot of suffering. That's the effect of counter-active karma. The rebirth was good. The karma necessary for rebirth as a human being was wholesome, but if there is strong counter-active karma, it creates unpleasant situations. That works in reverse also. Suppose a being is reborn as an animal. That is bad reproductive karma; it is a lower rebirth. The counter-active karma can make that existence as an animal very pleasant, as is experienced by many pets that people have in America. These animals live in more comfort than many people in the world. That powerful karma counteracts the bad rebirth karma. It works both ways.

The last is called destructive karma. It stops the flow of the other forces. Suppose you shoot an arrow into the air. The arrow has a certain momentum and if unobstructed, will continue until it falls at a certain place in the distance. Destructive karma is like a powerful force which halts the arrow in mid-air, knocking it to the ground. There are beings who experience an early death. Their reproductive karma and supportive karma might have been good, but somehow, from some past action, powerful destructive karma brings down the flight of that arrow, stops the flow of the other karmic forces.

There's a story of a man in the Buddha's time which illustrates some of the workings of karma. He gave an offering of food to an arhant, a fully enlightened being. After making the offering he started regretting having given it. It is said that for seven lifetimes in a row, he was born as a millionaire as a result of having given the food. It is very powerful to make an offering to a fully enlightened being. But the result of his having had all those moments of regret caused this very rich man to live in a very miserly way, completely unable to enjoy the fruits of his wealth. Different kinds of karma bring different kinds of results depending on our changing states of mind.

Reproductive karma is important to understand, because it determines in which plane of existence we take birth. It is the karma operative in the last moment of life. In that dying moment called death consciousness, there are four kinds of rebirth karma which may arise.

The first is called weighty karma, which can be either wholesome or unwholesome. Unwholesome weighty karma is wounding a Buddha, killing a fully enlightened being, killing one's mother or father, or causing a division in the order of monks. Any of those take precedence over all other actions in determining rebirth. They must come to fruition. The wholesome weighty karma is if one has cultivated concentration and reached the level of absorption, and maintained it until the time of death. The result of that karma is rebirth in the Brahma worlds. It takes predominance over other actions. The other skillful weighty karma is the experience of the different stages of enlightenment. It does not determine precisely where one is reborn but it directs one's rebirth upwards. It closes off rebirth in the lower worlds.

The karma that works if there are no weighty deeds to bear fruit is called proximate karma, which means the karma of those actions done immediately before dying. In other words, if in your dying moments you should remember something good you have done, or somebody reminds you of wholesome acts, or near the death moment you perform a good act, it is that karma which determines rebirth. There was in the Buddha's time a murderer who, just as he was about to be hung, recalled the one time in his life he had given alms to Sariputra, the chief disciple of the Buddha. His last thought was of that gift. Even though he had committed so many unwholesome acts in this life, the result of the last wholesome mind moment was rebirth in the heaven worlds. It works the other way too. It is not that the good or bad karma which was accumulated does not follow us. Rather the proximate karma, the immediate deed or remembrance we have in the moment before death, takes precedence. It determines the next existence. But consciousness often gets very weak at the time of death and there may not be the ability to redirect the mind or purposely recall certain events.

If there is no proximate karma, then habitual karma becomes involved. The actions done repeatedly in our lifetime then come to mind at the moment of death. If somebody has done a lot of killing, that kind of thought is going to arise in the death moment as a result of this habitual karma. Or if someone has done many good deeds, has been generous, or has done a lot of meditation, it will happen that he remembers one of these acts or perhaps sees an image of himself sitting on his meditation cushion. Then it is that karma which will determine the next birth.

If there is no weighty karma, no proximate karma, no strong habitual karma, the fourth kind which determines rebirth is called random karma. We are all trailing infinite wholesome and unwholesome karma and if there is no strong habitual karma, then any deed we've done from any time in the past may come up in the dying moment.

An example of the workings of these kinds of karma is that of a herd of cattle living unpenned in a barn. When the door is opened in the morning, the first one out is going to be the strongest bull. He will just push his way out, pushing aside all the others. Suppose there is no strong bull. The next one out the door is going to be the cow which is nearest to the door. She's just going to slip right out. Suppose there is no one particularly near the door. Then the cow who normally goes out first, who is in the habit of leading the others, will go out first. And if there is no cow in the habit of going out first, then any one of the herd might be the first out the door. That's how karma works in our last moment: the weighty, the proximate, the habitual, the random.

There is one factor which keeps us going towards more and more light, toward higher and higher kinds of happiness, and that is mindfulness. Mindfulness results in wholesome weighty karma, enlightenment. Mindfulness also results in good proximate karma.

If we are sharply aware, just in the dying moment, the mind will be balanced and free of defilement. Mindfulness is a stong habitual karma. If it is practiced every day and stongly conditioned in us, it is going to arise in the death moment. The kind of awareness, the kind of mind that is being cultivated now is an extremely powerful force. It will be a determining factor in the kind of karma which operates in the death moment.

Question: *Can beings in lower worlds create karma? For example, can a dog create karma by being loving and gentle or mean and aggressive?*

Answer: All beings are creating karma, animals included. You can see some very aggressive animals. You can see fear, anger, hatred. There are some very beautiful animals, really cooled out. It all depends on the quality of mind.

Is there family karma?

There is something called collective karma. For example, any national policy that is undertaken creates a certain national karma. We share in the karma of others if we approve of their actions. If we mentally approve of what someone else is doing, then there is a karmic force generated. You can see how it works in time of war. Some people are approving of it, thus sharing in that karma. Other people are not approving at all; they don't share that collective karma. I had a friend in India who was from Holland. He was describing his family during the second world war. He said that somehow or other they always had enough food. Although the whole country was in a state of tremendous deprivation and lack of food, particular people here and there did not suffer so intensely. You can see collective karma working in people who do not share in or approve of unwholesome actions of a nation, or a group, and who then don't share in the result either; or in the approving of skillful acts and policies which then accumulates wholesome karma.

Sometimes the words and examples you use confuse me.

Forget the examples. Go to your experience of what it means to be mindful. When there is a thought in the mind, there are two alternatives: The thought can arise and you can be completely involved with it, not knowing that you're thinking. Or mindfulness can be present and the awareness that thinking is going on. When there is mindfulness with regard to thoughts and all other objects, they come and go, are clearly seen, and the mind stays balanced behind them.

With all the words that are used some you will tune into and some you won't: it doesn't matter. Use the words or concepts which clarify things for you; leave the rest. It's the experience of what's happening that's important, not the belief or acceptance in anything that's said. All understanding comes out of a silence of mind, not out of a commentary on what's going on.

Well, it's the icing on the cake that gets you to eat the cake.

Use whichever color icing appeals to you. And then eat the cake! There's a story which might be useful:

There was a Professor taking a sea voyage in a little boat and one night he goes up to an old sailor and says, "Hey old man, what do you know about oceanography?" The old sailor didn't even know what the word meant. The Professor said, "You've wasted a quarter of your life! Here you are, sailing on the sea, and you don't even know any oceanography." The next night the Professor goes up to the old man and says, "Hey old man, what do you know about meteorology?" Again, the old sailor had never heard of the word. "The science of the weather." "Ah, I don't know anything about that." "Oh, you've wasted half your life!" The next night the Professor goes up to the old man, "What do you know about astronomy?" "Nothing." "Here you are, out on the sea, and you need the stars to navigate and you don't know anything about astronomy. You've wasted three-quarters of your life." The next night the old sailor comes rushing up to the Professor and says,

"Professor, what do you know about swimology?" The Professor says, "Oh nothing, I've never learned to swim." "Ah, too bad, the boat is sinking. You've wasted all your life!"

It's the swimology which is important.

•

Instruction: Relaxing/ Sinking Mind

When there is pain somewhere in the body, there is often a tendency to tense elsewhere as a reaction. It is good to periodically relax the whole body, part by part, letting go of all the accumulated tension which may gather as a subtle reaction to unpleasant sensations. Then it becomes easier to sit back and again watch the flow.

Make use of the hours of resolution when you are not changing position to spend an hour with complete non-movement. This kind of resolution strengthens the mind in several ways. The effort and energy factor become very strong, and the stillness of body also strengthens the concentration and mindfulness. Generally, our body reacts to every little discomfort or unpleasant feeling with a slight change in position. We are usually unmindful of that whole process: feeling a little discomfort, then a slight shift of posture. By making the resolution not to move for an hour, we cannot avoid becoming aware of all these moments of unpleasantness and our conditioned reactions to them. The hours of resolution can be increased. If you feel comfortable with them, you can make that resolve at every sitting.

As concentration improves, it is sometimes possible for the mind to go into a pleasant dreamlike state. This is called sinking mind. You can sit a long time in that state. Be wakeful, don't let the mindfulness get out of focus. When you feel yourself going into a kind of dreamy state of mind, make the effort to sharpen the mindfulness so that it is clearly aware of what's happening in the moment. In that way, the wisdom factor is developed, experiencing the instantaneous arising and vanishing of thoughts, of sensations, of the breath, of states of mind. Don't allow the mind to fall into a sinking state. That may happen when the sittings get very long. Be watchful. This is the basis of wisdom. Stay clearly attentive.

EIGHTEENTH
EVENING

•

Purity and Happiness

There is a story by Mark Twain about a man going to heaven. When he arrived, he was given a pair of wings and a harp, and for a few days he used the wings as a way of moving about, and plucked on the strings of the harp trying to get some celestial music out of it. Both were pretty much of a bother, and finally he realized that in heaven you don't actually need wings to go anyplace; and simply by desiring heavenly music, the celestial musicians appear and commence to play. So he put down the wings and the harp, and began to enjoy himself.

Similarly, we sometimes limit ourselves by preconceptions of purity and happiness. We burden ourselves with unnecessary wings or halos or harps thinking that happiness consists of having certain things or acting in a certain way. When we leave aside our limited views it is possible to open up to deeper experiences of joy.

There are many different kinds of happiness and each one arises because of a certain level of purity. Sense pleasures are the first kind of happiness which it is possible to enjoy: seeing beautiful things and hearing beautiful sounds, experiencing delicious tastes and smells, having blissful sensations in the body. As human beings we have many moments of these sense pleasures and although they are transitory, still they create a kind of joy and light and happiness in us.

An even higher kind of sensual happiness has been described in the cosmology as certain heaven worlds where everything is beautiful and pleasant. Beings have luminous bodies of light without any pain or unpleasantness, and sport in pleasure groves with sensual delights to satisfy every kind of desire. There are palaces made of precious gems, celestial musicians, heavenly nymphs, and even celestial yogis. It is said that Maitreya, the coming Buddha, is now living in one of these heaven worlds, teaching the Dharma to many beings there. Celestial happiness is of a very high kind.

The path to this happiness of sense pleasures is through purity of conduct, the first stage of purification. Purity of conduct means practicing generosity, kingly giving, and the practice of the moral precepts, restraining greed, anger, and delusion. It's this kind of purity in action which is the cause of beings enjoying all kinds of sensual happiness both in the human realm and, as it is said, in celestial realms as well.

There is a higher kind of happiness than even the happiness of heaven. That is the happiness and bliss of concentration. A mind that has developed a strong degree of one-pointedness enjoys a supra-sensual ecstasy, far superior to fleeting sensual pleasures. It is a mind withdrawn from sense objects and totally absorbed in an object. It is a much more sustained bliss than the enjoyment of different sense objects which are coming and going rather quickly.

There are some states of mind which can be developed through the power of concentration which are called, "The Dwellings of Brahma," or "The Divine Abodes." They are called this because they are the qualities of mind of beings in the Brahma worlds; the very highest and most exalted realms which can be experienced.

The first of the divine abodes is universal lovingkindness. Not love for particular people out of attachment or possessiveness; rather a love radiating from the mind wishing happiness and peace and joy for all beings everywhere. A mind that has reached this stage of concentration is capable of projecting love infinitely in all directions.

The second of these qualities is compassion for the suffering of all beings—feeling and caring for the sorrow and pain of others.

The third "Divine Abode" is a quality called sympathetic joy, which means sharing and delighting in the happiness of others; being filled with joy when we see others happy. A contrast to perhaps more common states of envy or jealousy or competitiveness. The mind that takes delight in the joy of others is light and radiant.

The last of these four qualities is equanimity: the perfect balance of mind undisturbed by vicissitudes, ups and downs, joys and sorrows. A mind that stays balanced and even. The happiness of infinite love and compassion, infinite sympathetic joy and equanimity, begins to be experienced as the mind becomes more one-pointed. As purity of conduct has to do with our actions, purity of mind has to do with the power of concentration.

There is an even greater joy than that of the Brahma worlds of deep concentration. This is Vipassana happiness, or the happiness of insight. The mind which is seeing clearly, penetrating deeply into the nature of things, experiences the arising and passing away of phenomena very distinctly. Vipassana happiness is far superior to the others because in that clarity of vision there is a taste of freedom. It is not merely a sinking into sensual delights, nor an absorption into meditative trances or concentrated bliss. It's the happiness of clear perception where the mind becomes luminous, and conscious- . ness begins to shine in its clarity. It's like polishing a crystal goblet until it becomes clear and sparkling. Through the practice of awareness, of Vipassana, the mind can achieve that same luminosity, and enjoy the extraordinary feeling of happiness which comes from deep insight.

There is a stage of purity, called purity of view, which makes possible the arising of Vipassana happiness. Purity of view means freedom from the view or concept of self. All that we are is a process of mind and body unfolding, continually becoming. The Buddha once gave a short discourse which he called "The All." It's called "The All" because he described everything in six phrases.

"The eye and visible objects; the ear and sounds; the nose and smells; the tongue and tastes; the body and sensations; the mind and mental objects or ideas."

This is the all; there is nothing apart from that. Often the Buddha remarked how the entire world exists within our fathom-long body. Understanding these objects and their sense base is to understand how the six kinds of consciousness with their respective objects are continually arising and vanishing: the knowing of sight and sound, smell and taste, sensations and ideas. Our whole universe consists of a very rapid sequence of hearing, seeing, smelling, tasting, feeling sensations, and experiencing different mind objects. Six objects only, six kinds of consciousness knowing them: what we are is this continuity of process. There is no one behind it to whom it is happening. There is no abiding entity of which it can be said "this is I," because each consciousness and its object arise and vanish moment to moment.

There is a very succinct expression of this teaching given by the Buddha: "In what is seen, there must be just the seen; in what is heard, there must be just the heard; in what is sensed (smell, taste, or touch), there must be just what is sensed; in what is thought, there must be just what is thought." Nothing apart from that, no self to whom it is happening.

Seeing, hearing, tasting, smelling, sensations in the body, mental objects. Our whole existence is the continuity of these six processes. The names we give to things are many. Innumerable concepts describe our experience. But the eye sees only color and form; it does not see names. What the ear hears is sound. We give many names to the different kinds of sounds, but what is actually happening is that vibrations come into contact with the ear which causes hearing consciousness to arise. A very simple cause and effect relationship. There is no one home. The rapidity of the sequence gives the illusion that it is all happening to someone. When the mind is quiet, we begin to experience the purification of view in which our whole being is seen as just that continuity of process of knowing and object, free of the concept of self. And as the purification deepens, we become one with the flow instead of trying to hold on to it. Purity of view is the clarity of understanding which sees things just as they are, the beginning of a transforming vision. It is the happiness of our first real taste of freedom.

The understanding of how things are happening becomes the gateway to the very highest kind of happiness: the happiness of nirvana, enlightenment. It is the peace, the rest, the coolness beyond the mind-body process. And it is the great beauty of the Dharma that all the different kinds of happiness come to us when we direct ourselves towards the highest freedom.

Question: *How would you describe the happiness of nirvana?*

Answer: Three kinds of happiness are experienced in nirvana. These can be considered as different aspects of the joy which comes from the end of suffering, the total cessation of pain.

When we were living in India we lived on the top of a mountain, and the bazaar, the shopping area, was about half an hour's walk down the mountain on a rather steep path. Things were mostly carried on one's back. There were a number of old Tibetan women who were carrying huge beams of timber up the mountain. They were trudging, bent over double, carrying this load on their backs all the way up the path. Imagine the feeling of ease when they reached the top and could lay down the load! A tremendous feeling of happiness to be relieved of such a burden.

The happiness of nirvana is release from the burden of suffering. It is the highest kind of happiness. By way of having a clear idea of what is involved in the path and what the experience of enlightenment entails, it might be helpful to elucidate the different kinds of nirvanic happiness and how they function.

The first of these is the culmination of the happiness of insight, of wisdom, of clear seeing, called path consciousness. The first glimpse of nirvana, the first experience of nirvana. This path consciousness has the function to uproot defilements like a bolt of lightning. It is not merely the suppression of defilements which happens in concentration, but the complete uprooting, the complete eradication of certain fetters of mind. In the very first glimpse, three of the ten fetters which bind us to samsara are eliminated. They are doubt, belief in rites and rituals (as a way of experiencing enlightenment), and the belief in self. These are completely uprooted from the continuity of consciousness by this single instant of path consciousness which has nirvana as the object.

Immediately following that comes the second kind of nirvanic happiness called fruition consciousness. One experiences the fruit of the path moment, also with the object being nirvana. In this fruition state, there is nothing further being uprooted; this happened in the first moment. The fruition state is the experience of nirvanic peace. Those who have developed a strong one-pointedness can go into the nirvana fruition state at will. They sit down and resolve to go into this state for half an hour or an hour or one or two days. It is said one can remain in this nirvanic peace for up to seven days at a time. Stillness, coolness, relief, freedom. Then one comes out of the fruition state and, because there are further defilements still latent in the mind, again one has to walk the path of insight. Just as we are doing now, the practice is continued. You see the rising and falling of all phenomena, you go through all the stages. You experience the second path consciousness moment, which eliminates further defilements. There are four occurrences of path moments which one by one eliminate the fetters which keep us bound to the wheel.

The highest kind of nirvanic experience is called parinirvana: the state when a fully enlightened being dies. There is no more rebirth, no more fuel, no more impetus to take birth again. It is like a great raging fire going out. The outness of the fire, the outness of the burning is a state of peace and silence and coolness. The very highest kind of happiness. Sometimes people worry about going out too quickly, wanting to enjoy one more movie, or one more sense delight, or spend a little time in heaven. If you aim for the highest happiness, all the other kinds of happiness come.

Is it possible after being born a human to take rebirth in the animal world? Can you get back again?

The reason that human birth is so extraordinarily precious is that once one has taken rebirth in one of the lower planes of existence it is said to be incredibly difficult to again experience a higher rebirth. It is not impossible, but it takes a very long time. The Buddha gave an example of the length of time involved. Suppose there is a blind turtle at the bottom of a great ocean. Somewhere on the surface of the ocean is a ring of wood floating on the waves, with the wind blowing it back and forth. The blind turtle surfaces once every hundred years. The chances that the blind turtle will put his head through the ring of wood are greater than the chances of a being in a lower world taking a human birth. This why our life now is so very precious and should not be wasted.

I have a hard time understanding how one can know what happens before birth and after death.

There are two ways of understanding this. The way we can relate to it best is understanding how the process works moment to moment. How birth and death are happening every instant, how consciousness arises and passes away. The passing away of consciousness is death. There is nothing of that consciousness which carries over to the next moment. Through the experience of insight, through meditation, we can experience momentary life and death; this offers an intuitive understanding of death and rebirth consciousness happening in exactly the same way. It is also possible, through the development of deep concentrated states, to develop all kinds of psychic power. Many beings of all religious traditions have developed these powers, and one of the abilities is not only to see other planes of existence but also to see beings dying and taking rebirth again. There are people who have this kind of vision. My teacher, in talking about all this, would go into the explanation of the heaven worlds and all the possibilities of psychic power, but he would always end by saying, "You don't have to believe it. It's so, but you don't have to believe it." There is no belief at all which has to be accepted in developing insight into who we are. Wisdom comes simply by being aware in a precise and penetrating way, free of all beliefs and concepts.

•

Devotion

One of the spiritual faculties, and a powerful help along the path, is faith or confidence. When we have faith in what we're doing, all the nagging doubts which can waylay our efforts become inoperative.

There are several different kinds of faith which may arise. The least skillful is that trust or devotion in someone or something simply because it makes us feel good. We get a pleasant feeling, a high, and so put our faith in that person or thing. It is easy for that kind of devotion to become blind. A higher kind of faith arises when we experience and appreciate certain qualities in a person such as wisdom and love and compassion. This kind of confidence is helpful because the appreciation is a recognition of wholesome qualities of mind which inspire us to develop those same qualities in ourselves.

There is also the faith and devotion that comes from our own experience of the truth. As we begin to experience on deeper levels how the mind and body are working, we feel a tremendous joy and confidence in the Dharma. It is not based on blind feelings nor on appreciation of qualities in another but comes from insight into the nature of reality. And this leads to the highest confidence of mind which comes from the experience of enlightenment. By penetrating to the ultimate truth, faith becomes unshakeable.

As the Buddha was dying, Ananda asked who would be their teacher after his death. He replied to his disciple: "Be lamps unto yourselves. Be refuges to yourselves. Take yourselves to no external refuge. Hold fast to the truth as a lamp. Hold fast to the truth as a refuge. Look not for a refuge in anyone besides yourselves. And those, Ananda, who either now or after I am dead, shall be a lamp unto themselves, shall betake themselves to no external refuge, but holding fast to the truth as their lamp, holding fast to the truth as their refuge, shall not look for refuge to anyone besides themselves, it is they who shall reach to the very topmost height; but they must be anxious to learn."

TWENTYFIRST EVENING

•

Dependent Origination

It is because of the mystery of birth, old age and death that Buddhas arise in the world. There is no realm of existence in which these realities do not exist, and it is the sole purpose of the Buddha's enlightenment to penetrate into their root causes. Perhaps the most profound part of the Buddha's teaching is the description of how this wheel of life, death and rebirth continues rolling on. The insight into all the links of the chain of existence is expressed in what is called the Law of Dependent Origination.

There are twelve links in this Law of Dependent Origination. The first two have to do with causes in the last life which condition birth in this one. The first of these links is ignorance. Ignorance means not knowing the truth, not understanding the Dharma, ignorance of the four noble truths. Because we do not perceive things clearly, because we do not perceive the fact of suffering and its cause and the way out, that force of ignorance conditions the next link in the chain: volitional actions of body, speech, and mind motivated by wholesome or unwholesome mental factors. Volitional activity is conditioned by ignorance; because we don't understand the truth, we are involved in all kinds of actions. And the karmic force of these actions conditions the third link in the chain.

The third link is rebirth consciousness; that is, the first moment of consciousness in this life. Because ignorance conditioned the energy of karmic activity in our last life, rebirth consciousness arises at the moment of conception. Volition or intention is like the seed; rebirth consciousness, like the sprouting of that seed. A cause and effect conditioned relationship. Because of ignorance there were all kinds of actions, all kinds of karmic formations. Because of karmic formations arises rebirth consciousness, the beginning of this life. Because of the first moment of consciousness in this life, arise the whole mind-body phenomena, all the elements of matter, all the factors of mind. Because of the mind-body phenomena arising, the sense spheres develop. This is during development of the embryo, before birth.

Rebirth consciousness at the moment of conception conditions the arising of mind-body phenomena. Because of that arise all the six spheres of the senses, the five physical senses and the mind, which in turn conditions the arising of contact, contact between the sense organ and its appropriate object: the eye and color, the ear and sound, nose and smell, tongue and taste, body and sensation, mind and thoughts or ideas. Contact involves the coming together of an object through its appropriate sense door and the consciousness of either seeing, hearing, smelling, tasting, touching, or thinking. Conditioned by the senses, contact comes into being. Because of the contact between the eye and color, the ear and sound, and the other senses and their objects, there arises feeling. Feeling means the quality of pleasantness, unpleasantness, or neither pleasantness nor unpleasantness involved in every mind moment, in every moment of contact. Whether it is contact through the five physical sense doors or through the mind, feeling is always present, and is called, therefore, a common mental factor. Conditioned by contact, there arises feeling; that is, the quality of pleasantness, unpleasantness or neutrality.

Because of feeling arises craving. Craving means desiring, hankering after objects. What is it that we desire? We desire pleasant sights and sounds, pleasant tastes and smells, pleasant touch sensations and thoughts, or we desire to get rid of unpleasant objects. Desire arises because of feelings. We start hankering after, or wishing to avoid, these six different objects in the world. Feeling conditions desire. Desire conditions grasping. Because we have a desire for the objects of the six senses, mind included, we grasp, we latch on to, we become attached. Grasping is conditioned by desire.

Because of grasping, again we get involved in karmic formations, repeating the kinds of volitions which, in our past life, produced the rebirth consciousness of this life. Feeling conditions desire, desire conditions grasping, and grasping conditions the continual actions of becoming, creating the energy which is the seed for rebirth consciousness in the next life. Because of these karmic actions resulting from grasping, again there is birth.

Because there is birth, there is disease, there is sorrow. There is decay, there is pain. There is suffering. There is death. And so the wheel goes on and on, an impersonal chain of causality.

The Buddha's problem, and the problem of us all, is to discover the way out of this cycle of conditioning. It is said that on the night of his enlightenment he worked backward through the Law of Dependent Origination, seeking the place of release. Why is there old age, disease and death? Because of birth. Why is there birth? Because of all the actions of becoming, all the volitional activities motivated by greed, hatred and delusion. Why are we involved in these kinds of activities? Because of grasping. Why is there grasping? Because of desire in the mind. Why is there desire? Because of feeling, because the quality of pleasantness or unpleasantness arises. Why is there feeling? Because of contact. Why is there contact? Because of the sense-spheres and the whole mind-body phenomena.

But there's nothing we can do now about being a mind-body process. That is conditioned by past ignorance and having taken birth. So there is no way to avoid contact. There's no possible way of

119

closing off all the sense organs even if that were desirable. If there's contact, there's no way of preventing feeling from arising. Because of contact, feeling will be there. It's a common factor of mind. But, it is right at this point that the chain can be broken.

Understanding the Law of Dependent Origination, how because of one thing, something else arises, we can begin to break the chain of conditioning. When pleasant things arise, we don't cling. When unpleasant things arise, we don't condemn. When neutral things arise, we're not forgetful. The Buddha said that the way of forgetfulness is the way of death. And that the way of wisdom and awareness is the path to the deathless. We are free to break this chain, to free ourselves from conditioned reactions. It takes a powerful mindfulness in every moment not to allow feelings to generate desire.

When there's ignorance in the mind, feeling conditions desire. If there's something pleasant, we want it; something unpleasant, we desire to get rid of it. But if instead of ignorance in the mind there is wisdom and awareness, then we experience feeling but don't compulsively or habitually grasp or push away. If the feelings are pleasant, we experience them mindfully without clinging. If unpleasant, we experience them mindfully without condemning. No longer do feelings condition desire; instead, there is mindfulness, detachment, letting go. When there is no desire, there's no grasping; without grasping, there's no volitional activity of becoming. If we are not generating that energy, there's no rebirth, no disease, no old age, no death. We become free. No longer driven on by ignorance and desire, the whole mass of suffering is brought to an end.

Every moment of awareness is a hammer stroke on this chain of conditioning. Striking it with the force of wisdom and awareness, the chain gets weaker and weaker until it breaks. What we are doing here is penetrating into the truth of the Law of Dependent Origination, and freeing our minds from it.

Question: *I am finding that as I practice I am becoming more and more aware of the beauty of the Dharma, the way things are working.*

Answer: The highest kind of happiness is Vipassana happiness, the happiness of insight, seeing how things are working. It is a very happy state when one begins to appreciate with a beginner's mind every moment as new, as fresh. So there is a great delight in existence which comes from a beginner's mind, from a de-conditioned mind, a mind that is experiencing directly rather than thinking about everything. The Buddha has said that the taste of the Dharma excels all other tastes. It gives such a feeling of clarity and understanding and beauty, to see clearly how everything is working, to be in tune, to be in harmony, to be one with the Tao.

On the way to the perfection of harmony is a very deep experience of the unsatisfactoriness, of the suffering inherent in this imperma-nent process. Many people here have had tastes of that dissatisfac-tion. Going through this perspective fosters tremendous detach-ment. When you deeply experience the suffering of mind and body, you see clearly the value of letting go, you're not grasping any more. You see nothing very desirable about it. Out of that kind of detachment, one's mind comes into a harmonious balance where you are seeing the whole flow with great equanimity, with a very clear and peaceful mind.

To achieve enlightenment, do you have to die?

Enlightenment is the death of greed, hatred and delusion. The reason that we have fear of dying is because we don't understand how the process is happening right now, and so to an untrained mind there's fear involved in giving this up. Actually, there is no one to die because there is no one behind the process. What is happening is moment to moment birth and death, birth and death. . .kept going by the force of desire and grasping. To decondition, to free the mind from grasping and desire, is to experience the state of peace which is there all the time but which we are prevented from realizing by the force of attachment. It's like that monkey who's holding on and nothing is binding him except the force of desire in his own mind. All he has to do is open his hand and slip out. All we have to do is let go.

TWENTYSECOND EVENING

•

Death and Lovingkindness

An image often used to describe the practice of insight is that of walking a tightrope. As we're walking the tightrope, it becomes clear that the one thing we must pay attention to is balance: maintaining perfect poise. While walking on the tightrope, different things come whizzing by us, different sights, and sounds, emotions, ideas, and realizations. If these are pleasant, the conditioned tendency of mind is to reach out, trying to hold onto them, trying to make them stay. If the sights and sounds are unpleasant, the tendency of mind is to reach out in aversion, trying to push them away. In both cases we reach out, and in the reaching, lose our balance and fall.

Both the positive and negative reactions are equally dangerous. Anything at all, however glorious or terrifying, which causes us to lose the perfect balance of mind, makes us fall. So we work again and again to develop a mind which doesn't react with clinging or condemning, attachment or aversion, to any of these objects. Developing a mind which clings to nought, to absolutely nothing whatever, just allowing it all to come and pass away.

Non-attachment grows out of deep insight into impermanence.

On one level this insight is recognizing the inevitability and imminence of our death. In the Bhagavad-Gita the question is asked, "Of all the world's wonders, which is the most wonderful?" The answer, "That no man, though he sees others dying all around him, believes that he himself will die."

Often, in forgetfulness of our destiny, we become over-involved in collecting things, in attachments and possessions, in wanting to become someone special. We get involved in many of the activities of little mind, taking our ambitions, our desires, ourselves, very seriously. We lose the perspective of big mind, we lose the perspective of death.

Don Juan uses this as a powerful teaching when he talks about using death as an advisor; keeping an awareness of one's impending death without remorse or sadness or worrying, but with clarity and acceptance. The recollection of our death lends power and grace and fullness to every moment, every action.

Each of us has deeply ingrained patterns which bear witness to everything we do; often these are destructive habits like anger or self-pity. But in just the same way we can learn to keep in mind the awareness of death, and have it bear witness to all of our actions. If we take death as our advisor, we live each moment with the power and fullness we would give to our last endeavor on earth.

When we keep death at our fingertips we become less involved, less compulsive about the satisfaction or gratification of various desires in the moment. When not so clouded by desires and fantasies, we're less inclined to hold onto things and more open to love and generosity. The awareness of death provides the space of clarity in which we can understand the process of who it is that we are, and who it is that dies.

Insight into impermanence on this level is the awareness of the transitory, temporal nature of all phenomena from moment to moment. In every moment the mind-body process, our entire universe, is arising and passing away, dying and being reborn. We

124

work on developing a mind that is silent and still, one that is unmoving in the face of such enormous change.

The whole practice evolves organically from simply being aware of what's happening in the present moment without reacting. One meditation teacher in India has said that all you have to do is sit, and know that you are sitting, and the whole of the Dharma will be revealed. You'll clearly see the unfolding of the laws of nature, and then the Dharma truly becomes your own.

During this organic evolution, born of balance and detachment, many beautiful and freeing qualities of mind begin to manifest. One of these qualities is love (metta). Love for oneself, in the sense of being allowing and non-judging, having a spaciousness and a lightness in the mind, and a strong lovingkindness toward others, not relating in terms of grasping or need or attachment. It's not a conditioned love—loving someone because of certain characteristics or attributes which they have, and if these change, then not feeling love for them anymore; it's not "businessman's love"—"I'll love you if you'll love me back."

The love that comes from wisdom is an unconditional, universal lovingkindness—a feeling of friendliness and warmth for all beings everywhere. Not just for those in a particular relationship to us, but a truly boundless feeling. Not looking to others for completion, not relating out of need, but radiating this infinite quality of love.

Another quality which begins to manifest strongly is compassion. This isn't self-pity or pity for others. It's really feeling one's own pain and recognizing the pain of others. The Pali word "kilesa," which is usually translated as defilement, more specifically means "torments of mind." The experience of anger, of greed, of all defilements, is a painful one, which becomes clear if we observe them when they arise and see how they affect our minds and bodies. As we grow in an understanding of the Dharma, we feel compassion for ourselves when they arise, rather than feel judgment and self-condemnation, and we recognize the pain others are experiencing when these states arise within them. Seeing the web of suffering we're all entangled in, we become kind and compassionate to one another.

The highest manifestation of these qualities comes as the expression of emptiness—emptiness of self. When there is no "I," there is no "other"; that feeling of separation disappears, and we experience a oneness, a unity of all things.

Albert Einstein wrote, "A human being is a part of the whole called by us universe, a part limited in time and space. He experiences himself, his thoughts and feelings as something separated from the rest, a kind of optical delusion of his consciousness. This delusion is a kind of prison for us, restricting us to our personal desires and to affection for a few persons nearest to us. Our task must be to free ourselves from this prison by widening our circle of compassion to embrace all living creatures and the whole of nature in its beauty."

Clouds of greed, hatred and delusion obscure the natural radiance of love and compassion in our minds. As we clear away these clouds through the unfolding of insight, the qualities of lovingkindness begin to shine forth naturally.

There is a specific practice which the Buddha taught to make these states of mind a powerful force in our lives. It's called "metta bhavana," or cultivation of lovingkindness. Doing this practice enriches Vipassana because of the spaciousness and lightness it creates in the mind. It strengthens the ability to see without judging, and helps us avoid the very common tendency in spiritual practice to condemn who we are and seek in a grasping way to be someone else.

All along the way you see that the means and the end are the same. To reach an end of peace and balanced awareness and love we work on expressing these factors in each moment.

Usually we practice lovingkindness meditation for about five or ten minutes at the beginning or the end (or sometimes both) of a sitting. In the beginning, it creates a space of acceptance which we carry over into the bare attention, and at the end the loving thought is often more powerful because the mind is concentrated.

The method is very simple. Sit in a comfortable position. As a way of freeing the mind from any tensions or grudges, begin by asking for and extending forgiveness: "If I have hurt or offended anyone in thought or word or deed, I ask forgiveness. And I freely forgive anyone who may have hurt or offended me." Repeating this silently once or twice is an effective way of clearing the mind of any residue of ill will or resentment.

Then for a few minutes direct phrases of loving thought towards yourself: "May I be happy, may I be peaceful, may I be free of suffering, may I be happy, peaceful, free of suffering," concentrating on the meaning of the words. It's difficult to have a genuine love for others until we can be accepting and loving of ourselves. The particular words which are used do not matter. Choose some phrases which resonate within you. It becomes a mantra of love.

Continue the practice beginning to extend these thoughts and feelings towards others: "As I want to be happy, so may all beings be happy. As I want to be peaceful, so may all beings be peaceful. As I want to be free of suffering, so may all beings be free of suffering." Repeating this in the mind a few times, begin to radiate the lovingkindness outward towards all beings. The phrases can be condensed into a rythmic repetition continuing for five or ten minutes: "May all beings be happy, peaceful, free of suffering."

You can also direct these thoughts to particular people, either those you are very close and for whom you already have a lot of love, or those towards whom you may be feeling anger or annoyance, as a way of opening to them with gentleness. Visualize them in the mind as you repeat the words. At the end, again generate the thoughts of lovingkindness towards all beings everywhere.

Although at first it may seem a mechanical exercise, as you practice, trying to concentrate on the meaning of the words, on what

127

it is that you are wishing for all others, slowly the feelings of love and compassion will grow and become strong.

Question: *Could you say a little more about how metta or love and insight are combined?*

Answer: The development of lovingkindness is a concentration technique, making the mind one-pointed in the feeling of love. It works on the conceptual level, with the concept of "being." It is a highly skillful use of the concept and it creates a space in which mindfulness works with much greater clarity. It is using concentration to develop a lightness of mind in order to penetrate to yet deeper levels of understanding.

Could you say something more about clarity?

You may have experienced times in the meditation when the mind is sharp and clear, picking up moment to moment what it is that's happening. The edges are clearly defined, as opposed to times of confusion or lack of clarity when you can't quite see things distinctly, and everything is a little hazy. It's like a room in dim light: if we turn on a strong light, everything becomes sharp and clear. When there's just a little light in the mind, you can't see things so clearly, you get the general outlines, but without that sharp perception. With a lot of light in the mind, everything becomes distinct; then the process becomes so clear, so easy to understand. That light is the light of awareness, of mindfulness.

You don't become attached to that clarity?

You can. That is called a corruption of insight. You have to become aware of the clarity itself so as not to cling to it, not to identify with it. Because clarity is just part of the process also. When mindfulness and concentration first become strong it is common for people at that point to think they're enlightened, that there's nothing more to do. It feels so good and there's so much light and love and joy and calm and peace. That's where a teacher is a big help just to say, "Keep sitting."

Does the clarity stay with you through the changes or is it just another thing that comes and goes?

As the practice develops, it stays more and more, although certainly not without interruption. It's a factor of mind which gets stronger the more you practice. You go through progressive stages of clarity even when there's no longer the joy and rapture. There can be clarity in states of suffering. You go through periods where you experience the tremendous suffering of the process as well as the joy. There can be clarity in both. The path, as Don Juan said, is to arrive at the totality of oneself. Not to experience just one part but to experience the happiness, the sorrow, the clarity, everything. To really see the totality of who we are.

Does the lovingkindness meditation only affect our own mind space?

The power of a loving thought when directed by a highly concentrated mind is very great. There is a story about the Buddha and his cousin, Devadatta, who wanted to kill the Buddha and become head of the order of monks. Devadatta knew he could not kill the Buddha in any ordinary way, so he arranged to have a huge mad elephant charge down the lane where the Buddha was walking for alms. He thought that either the Buddha would run away and be discredited, or that he would be trampled to death. The next day as the Buddha was walking up the narrow road, Devadatta prodded the elephant to charge. The Buddha did not run away. He just stood there calmly, with a very concentrated mind, sending out powerful thoughts of love towards the charging elephant. It is said that the mind of the elephant was made completely tranquil by the Buddha's power of lovingkindness, and tradition has it that the elephant knelt down in the dust at his feet.

How is metta best expressed?

Compassion and love do not necessarily mean following a set course of action. It means doing one's best to act with love and compassion in a way that seems appropriate to the situation. The idea is not to look for a prescription for a specific action in every situation because you must be really honest with yourself, with what you are feeling. In the beginning, the practice of metta often seems mechanical. Metta is a factor of mind, not some mysterious thing we have or don't have. In this way, it is like mindfulness or concentration or wisdom or greed or anger. If you practice, it gets stronger, if you don't practice, it gets weaker. In the beginning, it's not effortless, it's not happening spontaneously, but as you develop it you become proficient in lovingkindness, and it starts happening by itself.

TWENTYFIFTH
EVENING

•

Tao

There is an ancient Taoist story about a tree. The tree was old and crooked; every branch twisted and gnarled. Somebody walking by that old and crooked tree commented to Chuang Tzu what a useless tree it was; because the trunk and branches were so crooked the tree served no purpose at all.

Chuang Tzu replied:

> The tree on the mountain height is its own enemy. . . . The cinnamon tree is edible: so it is cut down! The lacquer tree is profitable: they maim it. Every man knows how useful it is to be useful. No one seems to know how useful it is to be useless.

The uselessness of the tree is what protected it. Nobody wanted it for anything, so they didn't cut it down, and it lived to be very old, fulfilling its own nature.

"No one seems to know how useful it is to be useless." What does it mean to be useless? It means being empty of striving to become something, to be anything special, freeing the mind from that kind of gaining idea. To become useless is to settle back and allow our own nature to express itself in a simple and easy way.

There's a famous monk in Thailand who summed up this attitude of mind, and indeed the whole Dharma, in a very short saying. He said, "There's nothing to be, nothing to do, and nothing to have." Nothing special. Everything is impermanent, everything is in flow, in constant transformation. If we can free ourselves of the striving to be someone special, to be a certain way, or to have certain things— free of that desire to do or to be or to have anything at all—we can settle back into the natural unfolding of Dharma.

A lot of Taoist writings are about being invisible in the world. There is a story of a Chinese prince who went to hunt monkeys. When he came to the forest, the monkeys in the trees scattered very quickly. There was one monkey who didn't run away, he just sat on the end of a branch. The prince took his arrow and shot it, but with great agility the monkey caught the arrow in mid-air before it hit him. At that, the prince gave orders for all his huntsmen to shoot. They all shot their arrows at once and the monkey was killed.

Because the monkey was demonstrating his skill with defiance, taking pride in his trick, it became the cause of his destruction. In the same way, when we act with the idea in mind of some kind of show or demonstration of how good or smart or clever we are, or when there is any projection arising from the idea of self, that very action creates exactly the opposite forces, involving us in tension and conflict. To walk in the world invisibly means not aggressively asserting our skills or qualities, not making a show. It is an attitude of mind which operates without the sense of I, without the sense of self-importance, or self-striving. Just being in the moment in harmony with the situation.

One of the things that struck me most forcibly when I began the practice of meditation was the fact that so many actions were motivated by a desire to project some image: dressing a certain way, relating to people in a certain way; all revolving about a concept of myself I had created and then struggled to maintain. To carry around an image of ourselves is a great burden, causing a strain or tension between what we actually are in the moment and the image we're trying to project. It's not acting invisibly, it's not acting with that basic emptiness of self which is the settling back into the Dharma, into the Tao. There's nothing special to be, nothing special to do, nothing special to have. We can let go of self images, let go of projections, and all the tensions involved in sustaining them. Settling back and letting it all unfold by itself without any preconceptions of who we are.

Suzuki Roshi in his book *Zen Mind, Beginner's Mind* gives a good example for the ease and breadth of that kind of mind. He says that the best way to control a cow is to give it a big pasture. It's difficult to control a cow in a small and confined space. But if you give it a big pasture, then the very spaciousness of the place keeps it under control. In the same way, the best way to control the mind is to give it a wide range. There is no need to confine it or restrict it or restrain it in a narrow space. Settle back and let it be as it is, free of any striving, free of any idea of attaining anything. Give it a big pasture and watch the unfolding. The attitude of trying to get something, trying to become something, very often extends into spiritual practices as well. We have the idea of gaining something, which is a big hindrance to the practice. It's not understanding the emptiness of the unfolding, the emptiness of the Tao.

There's a writer by the name of Wei Wu Wei who expresses very succinctly this idea of settling back without striving. He says, "What we are looking for *is* what is looking." It's not something outside of us that we have to reach for or hold onto or attain. He said, "There's only one question, and the asking is the answer." The asking is what is happening in the moment. And that's the answer to the question. The answer is not something "out there" that we have to find or discover. The answer to the one big question of who we are is the asking of it.

This helps in understanding the Zen system of meditation and teaching which uses the koan, seemingly unsolvable problems. We give the mind a problem which has no rational answer, such as, "What is the sound of one hand clapping?" As long as we're looking for an answer by trying to solve the problem we don't understand the process. The asking of the problem, the asking of the koan, is the answer. And, in fact, the solution to the koan is not any particular answer at all. It's the ability to totally respond in the moment. That's what our whole practice is: being totally in the moment — in the asking, in the answering. Not seeking for solutions by wanting a certain state or having a certain kind of thought or conceptual understanding, but to be totally experiencing the process in the moment.

The biggest obstacles to settling back are attachments to self-images and concepts of who we are and how we want to be. They complicate unnecessarily the very simple experience of what it is that's happening. Often people on the spiritual path get trapped by an image. An image of what they think it means to be a yogi or a meditator or a spiritual person, creating for themselves that struggle of trying to live up to a certain preconceived way of action or behavior.

When I was studying in India I had three different teachers. Studying with each of them was an important lesson in understanding that there is no one way to be. Enlightenment is not expressed through any one kind of personality. These teachers were quite unalike in personality and style. Each one was an embodiment of wisdom, and love and power, without any image of how that embodiment should be expressed.

Wei Wu Wei said that humility is the absence of any one to be proud. It's not some stance of posture or personality. True humility is to be empty of self. My teachers displayed this "absence" each in their own natural way. To see the Dharma manifesting in so many

134

different ways was a great help in understanding there is no one way we have to be. There's no personality we have to assume in this process of purification. To settle back and let our personalities express themselves very naturally, to let the Dharma unfold. There's nothing to do and nothing to be and nothing to have. And with that state of mind we can do, we can be, and we can have freely.

There's a Zen story about staying free of concepts about oneself and others, in which a great Zen teacher is called on by the governor of Kyoto. His attendant presented a card which had his name followed by "Governor of Kyoto." "I have no business with such a person," said the Master, "tell him to get out of here." The attendant returned the card with apologies. "That was my error," said the Governor and scratched out the words, "Governor of Kyoto." "Ask the master again." "Oh, is that him," exclaimed the teacher when he saw the card, "I want to see that fellow."

When he presented himself as the "Governor of Kyoto," he was very far from the Dharma. When he presented himself as he was in the moment, free of an image, free of concept, he was just with what was happening and able to meet the great Zen master. To be able to relate to others without the boundaries of an image, makes possible very dynamic interactions. Often we put ourselves and others into little mental boxes or compartments—"Somebody is this way or that way, I know where they're at!" We relate in a very static way through the veil of concept. Everything is changing in each moment; our minds, our bodies, the situation around us. To stay fluid, to stay free of concepts and self-images, allows for these changes, and our understanding in relationships remains open and unencumbered.

So much of our lives centers around the idea of self, trying to fulfill it or satisfy it. This energy is carried over into spiritual practice by the kind of mind which is somehow trying to do battle with the ego, thinking the "self" is something to get rid of. Battling with the self does not reflect an understanding of how the process is happening.

Wei Wu Wei wrote a parable called, "The Goose":

Destroy the ego? Hound it, beat it, snub it, tell it where it gets off? Great fun, no doubt. But, where is it? Must you not find it first? Isn't there a word about catching your goose before you cook it?

The great difficulty here is that there isn't one.

All that effort, all that energy, to annihilate the ego. . .and it's not there in the first place. There's nothing to strive for and there's nothing to get rid of. We need only to stop creating the self in our minds in each moment. To be in the moment free of concept, free of image, free of clinging. To be simple and easy. There's no struggle or tension in that invisibility, in that effortlessness.

There is a beautiful poem describing the possibility of this way of living:

What is meant by a 'true man?' The true men of old were not afraid when they stood alone in their views. No great exploits. No plans. If they failed, no sorrow. No self congratulation in success. . .The true men of old slept without dreams, woke without worries. Their food was plain, they breathed deep. . .The true men of old knew no lust for life, no dread of death. Their entrance was without gladness, their exit yonder, without resistance. Easy come, easy go. They did not forget where from, nor ask where to. Nor drive grimly forward fighting their way through life. They took life as it came, gladly; took death as it came, without care; and went away, yonder. They had no mind to fight Tao. They did not try, by their own contriving, to help Tao along. These are the ones we call true men. Minds free, thoughts gone, brows clear, faces serene. Were they cool? Only cool as autumn. Were they hot? No hotter than spring. All that came of them came quiet, like the four seasons.

Question: *How can we make an effort without striving?*

Answer: The effort is exactly to be free of striving; settling back to be mindful in the moment. Some of you may have experienced, in the growth of awareness, not being caught up in projections or concepts. When the mind is in that space, there is nothing to do. When you sit down, it's just sitting, and you are effortlessly aware of whatever is happening.

It seems now that the perfect expression of my Dharma is to be an unmindful dreamer. But even being patient, I'm waiting for it to end, looking beyond it, it seems to be almost all I can do. . .

There is insight which comes from knowing that one is daydreaming. Having even a moment's glimpse of that wandering mind indicates the possibility of living uninvolved in those concepts and shadows.

How does choosing a livelihood come in?

It can all be done from the awareness of an appropriate need, rather than some expression of self. Instead of it being the fulfillment of some image we have of ourselves, we can just do what is appropriate in the moment, open to service and motivated by love and compassion. Then it flows simply and easily. Nothing special to do or to be or to have.

What about planning that has to be done?

The planning mind is happening in the moment. Be aware of the planning mind as an expression of the present moment. To be just with what's happening, using the thought process and the whole conceptual framework in dealing with the world, but staying grounded by realizing it's all just now. To act without attachment to the fruits of the action.

When I talk I have a lot of ideas about what I want to say. I'd like to know what it's like to really listen and talk mindfully?

There's only one way to find out. That's the message of the Zen koan. A Zen master gives his disciple the problem of Mu and there the student is, sitting on his cushion, going "Mu, Mu, Mu. . .What am I going to say to him when he asks me what's it all about?. . .Mu, Mu. . ." Or whatever the koan is. And he goes in for the interview with the master thinking all the time, "What am I going to say?" When the master asks him what he has discovered about Mu, he fumbles around with an answer. The master hits him over the head. He had not been at all in the present moment. The answer to the question is not an answer at all, except to be exactly in the moment. Any total response, empty of self, is the answer to the question. The asking is the answer. What we're seeking for is what is seeking. It's all right now in the moment. But our minds are always seeking an easy answer for someone to give us. When I know the answer, then I'll have "it." That's when you get hit over the head. Being hit over the head is in the present moment, it's right here.

What about listening to music?

Music is a good example of how, if you get out of the moment, you miss it! If you are listening to music and the mind starts thinking, the music doesn't stop for you; all the time you're thinking, you're not hearing. It can be a good training in staying with the flow of sound. Impermanence is so clear. Music is not a single thing but a continual arising and vanishing.

There seems to be a distinction between awareness and absorption in something. I can be engrossed in music, without being mindful; very much in the moment, but not being aware of being in the moment.

That's the difference between concentration and mindfulness. You can be very one-pointed on the music yet not very mindful, although there will be some mindfulness there. What is predominant is the one-pointedness factor, the mind not wavering. Add to that a sharp mindfulness and there you have the entire practice.

How do we purify ourselves?

The whole beauty of the practice is that the awareness itself is what purifies. It's not establishing a certain program for oneself, "I'm going to be pure," which is somewhat a contradiction. The awareness of what's happening in the moment is what purifies so that there's nothing to get or be, nothing special to do or have; just a sitting back with awareness.

Some of the greatest beings throughout the ages have offered teachings, written books, played music, created art and such; isn't all that an expression of themselves?

When you are invisible, when there's no desire to do or be anything, then in fact you can do or be or have anything at all. It's very true that many of the greatest enlightened beings, very spontaneously expressed their understanding, expressed the Dharma, through art and literature; but it was not with the attitude of demonstrating or showing anything. It was part of the unfolding, a very spontaneous and intuitive expression, not coming from the sense of I or self or "look at this." So many of the great masters were artists and poets; but that art, that creativity, came out of emptiness.

Can you still have a desire to do something, to help others, and have it not be selfish?

There is a semantic problem of using the word "desire" to reflect two different states. One is the desire of greed and grasping at something and the other is the desire of motivation. The desire of motivation can come out of emptiness, out of wisdom, out of love, compassion. This kind of motivation is very different than acts coming out of grasping, or the concept of self. The Buddha after his enlightenment, taught for forty-five years. There was a lot of doing involved, but no one behind it. It was an unfolding of Dharma. And so in our lives we will all unfold in our own ways, expressing our personalities, our own nature. If we can do it without the sense of, "I have to do this to become someone, to be famous or rich," just allowing it to unfold in the moment, then anything becomes possible. It's a tremendous opening into freedom. If we stay free of self-images and self-concepts, then we remain much more intuitive and responsive to changing situations. But if we have some idea of ourselves, of being a certain way, that concept acts as blinders, and we enter a very narrow path dictated by that particular image or concept, not at all responsive to changing circumstances around us. If we stay open and receptive, the whole process becomes one of harmonious interaction. There is no need to limit ourselves by a self-image. Stay fluid. Stay open.

•

Factors of Enlightenment

The Buddha described very clearly the path to liberation. This way to freedom consists in the development of seven mental factors which are called the seven factors of enlightenment. When all these different factors of mind are cultivated and brought to maturity, the mind becomes liberated from all kinds of bondage, from all kinds of suffering. All the various spiritual paths are concerned with the cultivation of one, another, or all of these seven limbs of freedom.

The first factor of enlightenment is mindfulness. Mindfulness is the quality of noticing, of being aware of what's happening in the moment, not allowing the mind to be forgetful. The Buddha said that he knew of no other factor which was as powerful as mindfulness for the cultivation of wholesome states of mind and the diminishing of unwholesome ones. There is nothing special we have to do to eliminate unskillful states or to make skillful ones happen, except to be aware of the moment. Awareness itself is the purifying force.

In a famous discourse, the Buddha said it is the cultivation of the four foundations of mindfulness which is the sole way to freedom. Awareness has been called by many different names in different traditions, but it is not the name which is important. It is the development of that kind of wakefulness, of alertness, of mindfulness, which is the way.

There are four foundations or applications of mindfulness. The first is mindfulness of the body: the breath, sensations, different movements and postures. Becoming aware and sensitive to all the changing aspects of our physical existence.

The second foundation of mindfulness is feeling, the quality of pleasantness, unpleasantness, or neutrality which arises with every moment of consciousness. With every object there is a corresponding feeling. When these feelings are predominant, when the quality of pleasantness or unpleasantness is strong, they become the objects of the meditation. Feelings are important because it is this factor which conditions our clinging and condemning. It is because of pleasant feelings that we desire objects. It is because of unpleasant feelings that the mind condemns, has aversion and hatred. The second application of mindfulness is to notice these feelings as they are arising and passing away, without clinging to the pleasant, without condemning the unpleasant.

The third foundation of mindfulness is consciousness. To be aware of the knowing faculty with all its concomitant mental states. When there is anger in the mind, to be aware of the angry mind; when there is lust, to be aware of the lusting mind, or the fearing mind. To be aware of consciousness as it is colored by all these different factors, without grasping or aversion, without judging, without evaluation or commenting. Anger is not I, not self, it is merely a mental state which colors the consciousness at that moment. Sit back and watch it arise and pass away. With the attitude of choiceless observation, no mental state has the power to disturb the mind. They are all part of a passing show. Nothing to be elated or depressed about. Simply to be mindful, to be aware.

The last of the four foundations is mindfulness of the Dharma, awareness of the truth, the law, awareness of the three characteristics of existence, and of the four noble truths. To see suffering, and the cause of suffering, the end of suffering, and the way to the end. To be mindful of these kinds of insights as they arise. Mindfulness of the Dharma.

There are many techniques of Vipassana, which may concentrate on one or more of these four fields of mindfulness. Observing any one of them will serve the purpose of bringing the mind to a state of clarity of vision, of balance. Depending upon temperament, upon personality, background, and conditioning, different techniques might suit different people. But the technique itself should not be clung to; what is important is the mindfulness which is being cultivated.

The second limb of enlightenment is called investigation of the Dharma. It is the quality of mind that is investigating, probing, analyzing the mind-body process, not with thoughts, not on the conceptual level, but with a silent and peaceful mind. It is intuitively and experientially investigating how the whole process is working. It is another name for the wisdom factor, that light in the mind which illuminates everything that is happening. When investigation is cultivated, it is seen that everything in our mind and body is in a state of flux. There is nothing permanent, everything is arising and vanishing continually. Both consciousness and objects are coming and going. There is nothing to take a stand on, no place to find security. Everything is in continual transformation. Through this factor of investigation, the experience of impermanence is deeply integrated in our understanding. We experience on the deepest levels that the mind is just a continual flow of phenomena, thoughts, images, emotions, moods; that the body is a collection of vibrations, of sensations, nothing solid, nothing to cling to. With this experience of impermanence comes a deep intuitive understanding that there is nothing in the mind-body process which is going to give lasting happiness. No lasting satisfaction, completion, or perfection is possible because it is all continually passing away. It is like trying to find happiness or security in a bubble of water. The instant it is touched, it is gone. Moment to moment dissolution. Inherently insecure. And along with the impermanence and unsatisfactory nature is also seen the emptiness of self. Nowhere in the mind and body is to be found any permanent entity which can be called self or I. There is no one behind the process to whom it refers.

"In the seeing, there is only what is seen; in the heard, only what is heard; in the sensed, there is only what is sensed; in the thought, there is only what is thought." There is only this flow of process. Seeing, hearing, smelling, tasting, touching and thinking. The sum total of our universe is these six processes. Empty phenomena rolling on. Empty of self, empty of I. All of these characteristics are experienced intuitively on a deep level, as the factor of investigation is cultivated. It is wisdom illuminating the mind.

One of the peripheral aids in the growth of the wisdom factor is said to be personal cleanliness, cleanliness of the body, of one's clothes, of one's surroundings. The example is given of a kerosene lamp. If the glass and wick and kerosene are all dirty, the light that comes from the lamp will not be very clear or bright. But if the glass is shining and the wick and kerosene are clean, the light that comes from the lamp will be very bright, and clear vision becomes easy.

The third factor of enlightenment is energy or effort. Nothing happens without effort. When we want to accomplish anything at all in the world, if we want money, or proficiency in some skill, there is a certain amount of effort that has to be put forth. What we are doing now is cultivating the very highest good. Effort and energy has to be put into it. The Buddha only points the way; we each have to walk upon the way ourselves. There is no one who can enlighten another being. The defilements of greed and hatred and delusion exist within our own minds. No one put them there. No one can take them out. We have to purify ourselves. Energy has to be aroused by each one of us to walk upon the path of purification. Energy is a powerful factor; when it is cultivated and developed it overcomes the sloth, torpor and laziness of mind. Whenever there are difficulties, problems along the way, the putting forth of effort rouses the whole system. It is a great support, an integral part of the path to freedom.

The fourth limb of enlightenment is rapture. Rapture means an intense interest in the object. It has been described as zestful joy. A joyous interest in what's happening. A simile given is of a person walking many days in a desert, very hot and tired, dirty and thirsty. Not too far in the distance, he sees a great lake of clear water. The interest his mind will take in that water, the joy he will feel, that's like the enlightenment factor of rapture. Rapture is a spaciousness in the mind born of detachment, free of grasping or clinging or identified involvement.

One way to cultivate this factor is reflecting about the ten perfections which characterize the Buddha's enlightenment. The perfection of generosity. Giving motivated by wanting to help ease the pain and suffering of all beings. The Buddha did not stop to wonder whether some people were worthy, and others not. Universal giving. The perfection of morality. The complete non-harming of all beings. Renunciation. Energy. Wisdom. Patience of mind, continual perseverance. Patience is a great virtue on the spiritual path. Lovingkindness. Truthfulness. Resolution. Equanimity. All these spiritual qualities were brought to perfection in the enlightenment of the Buddha. We can make the factor of rapture grow in our minds when we contemplate the Buddha and reflect that we too are cultivating the same qualities. In all acts of giving, in every act of patience, of truthfulness, and the rest, we are sharing in the perfection of Buddhahood. The reflection on our own development, our own wholesome actions, brings joy to the mind. Thinking about the Dharma: reflecting on the four noble truths, on the fact of impermanence, or selflessness—all timeless characteristics of existence, true for all people at all times. Reflection about the truth of the Dharma, through our own experience of it and its inviting quality of "come

145

and see," rather than "you must believe." The appreciation of the law, of the Tao, brings a great joy to the mind and cultivates the factor of rapture. Intense delight in exploring the truth creates a very light and buoyant state of mind.

The fifth factor of enlightenment is calm. An example given of this kind of tranquility is of someone coming out of the hot sun into the shade of a big tree. The coolness which that person feels is like the factor of calm, when all the passions are subdued, a cooled out mind not burning with lust or anger.

The sixth factor of enlightenment is concentration. Concentration means the ability of the mind to stay one-pointed on an object, to stay steady without flickering or wavering. The mind that is not concentrated stays superficial, floating from object to object. Concentration gives strength and penetrating power to the mind. There are two kinds of concentration. One is developed by focusing on any single object, and developing concentration to the point of absorption into it. This kind of one-pointedness becomes the basis of many psychic powers. The other form of concentration, the kind used for the development of insight, is called momentary concentration. It is a mind which is steady and one-pointed on changing objects. It is this kind of concentration which, in conjunction with all the other factors of enlightenment, leads to freedom.

The last limb of enlightenment is equanimity. Equanimity means evenness of mind. When things are going well, there is no wild elation. When things are not going well, there is no depression. Equanimity is an impartiality towards all phenomena, treating all phenomena equally. The example given of equanimity is that of the sun which shines upon the earth. The sun does not choose to shine upon some things and not upon others. It shines upon everything equally. The factor of equanimity is acceptance and receptivity towards all objects. One kind of reflection which cultivates this factor of equanimity, especially in dealings with others, is remembering that all beings are the heirs, the inheritors, of their own past karma. So when we see beings in great happiness, we can appreciate and find joy in their happiness, but with an equanimous mind, knowing that they are reaping the fruits of their own past deeds. Or when we see beings in suffering, we can feel compassion, and work to alleviate the suffering, but with an evenness of mind, knowing that it is the working out of the law, of the Dharma. Equanimity is not indifference, but rather a strong balance of mind. In meditation, when the mind starts to be aware on a microscopic level of the instantaneously changing process, it is this factor of equanimity which keeps everything in balance, in perfect poise.

These are the seven qualities of enlightenment that have to be brought to maturity in our practice. Three of them are arousing factors, and three are tranquilizing ones. Wisdom, energy and rapture all arouse the mind; they make it wakeful and alert. Calm, concentration and equanimity tranquilize the mind and make it still. They all have to be in harmony: if there is too much arousal, the mind becomes restless; if too much tranquility it goes to sleep. The factor of mindfulness is so powerful because it not only serves to awaken and strengthen all the other factors, but it also keeps them in their proper balance.

The evolution of mind along this path can fill one with tremendous inspiration and encouragement. Imagine a mind that has brought to full development mindfulness and wisdom, energy, rapture, calm, concentration, and equanimity. It is a mind which is shining and full of joy. That is what we are doing. Not only do the factors of enlightenment bring happiness in the moment, but all of them slope towards nirvana, towards enlightenment, towards freedom.

Sometimes from day to day, it is easy to forget what it is we are doing in dealing with the restlessness and pains and aches and wandering mind. But what is happening imperceptibly from moment to moment, but very progressively, surely, and steadily, is the development and growth of these limbs of enlightenment. It's a very great thing that is being done. It is the noblest evolution of mind.

Question: *Is enlightenment gradual or does it come as a sudden flash?*
Answer: It's both. Enlightenment is always sudden in the sense that it's an intuitive understanding. It's not something that you can think out. It comes out of a silent mind, an intuitive, sudden, wordless understanding. But that kind of intuitive understanding doesn't happen by accident. There's a certain balance of mind which has been cultivated making that sudden understanding possible.

And then from that understanding does the person then act accordingly? It seems that now I get some understanding, but I don't seem to act on it.
Just the fact of being slightly more aware changes the way in which you act. The awareness is very powerful. Once you've had a glimpse of just watching what's going on, it's very difficult to get caught up in quite the same old way, even when we're involved in the same actions again. It's like some little voice in the background saying, "What are you doing?" That little bit of awareness which has been cultivated acts as a powerful force. And slowly the understanding gets more totally integrated into our actions.

I have a question about the impermanence of happiness. There are people in the world who are intensely in love with God and they seem to constantly emanate a joy.
This is to be understood in two ways: first, all states are momentarily impermanent; that is, happiness is not constant in the mind because the mind itself is arising and vanishing in every moment. So in that very fundamental sense, on the mind-moment level, it's impermanent. There is nothing steady, nothing static. In the second sense, there are people who cultivate a love of God, who

cultivate union with God, God-realization, through the development of concentration. They may enjoy a long period of that kind of happiness. Even though it is in process, it is a rather continuous state. But that also, as a long term state of affairs, is impermanent. As long as the conditions are there for that love of God, or as long as concentration is cultivated, then it bears its karmic rewards. But, if there is any ignorance latent in the mind, that bliss will continue only as long as the force of concentration is behind it, and then again the mind will return to states colored by hatred, greed, and delusion. Through the force of a concentrated mind, the defilements can be suppressed, and for the time that one is concentrated, everything is fine and happy. As soon as the mind comes out of that state of concentrated bliss, those factors which have been held down, which have been suppressed in the mind, again become operative. That is why it is important to completely uproot the defilements through insight so they are no longer able to arise in the mind.

With all his compassion, why doesn't a Buddha stay around and help others?

A Buddha is the embodiment of the Dharma, the law; he is not apart from the workings of it. Having taken birth, decay and death must inevitably follow. Whether you are enlightened or unenlightened, this is part of the natural unfolding. But the truth itself is timeless, and having been shown the path to understanding, we need not rely on anyone outside of ourselves.

I noticed that love wasn't one of the factors of enlightenment. What about the danger of one remaining dry and cold?

It is important to understand the different meanings of love. The first level is the kind we discussed before, businessman's love. We love someone for something in return. The second kind of love is a wishing well towards all beings, a universal lovingkindness, wishing happiness and joy to all beings everywhere. That's an unlimited and unconditional kind of love. But it still deals with concepts, that is, the concepts of man, woman, being. These concepts are not ultimate realities. What we ultimately are is a collection of elements arising and passing away in every moment. There is a third kind of love, higher even than universal lovingkindness. This love is the natural harmony which comes from the breaking down of barriers arising out of the concept of self. No "I," no "other." It is love born of wisdom and at this level, "love" and "emptiness" are the same experience. There is no concept at all of "I am loving." It's free of the concept of I, of self. When you experience the highest level of love, you express all the other levels as well. Look around at the high teachers you know. They are full of love and light, but not with any thought that they should be that way; it's the natural expression of the Dharma.

•

Buddhist Paths

The Buddha did not teach Buddhism. He taught the Dharma, the law. He did not teach a set of beliefs or dogmas, or systems that have arbitrarily to be accepted. Through his own experience of enlightenment, he pointed the way for each of us to experience the truth within ourselves. During the forty five years of his teaching, he used many different words and concepts to point to the truth. The words or concepts are not the truth itself; they are merely a pointing to a certain kind of experience. In the Buddha's time, because of the force of his wisdom and skill, generally people did not confuse the words for the experience. They heard what the Buddha had to say, looked within, and experienced the truth in their own minds and bodies.

As time went on and people started to practice less, they began to mistake the words for the experience. Different schools arose, arguing over concepts. It is as if in attempting to explain the light on a full moon night one points up at the moon. To look at the finger, rather than the moon, is to misunderstand the pointing. We should not confuse the finger for the moon, not confuse the words pointing to the truth for the experience itself.

151

When the Dharma was brought to China, it evolved in a special way, with an intermingling of Buddhist and Taoist teachings. One of the people who most influenced the direction and expression of this Ch'an (later Zen) school was the sixth Chinese Patriarch, Hui Neng. Although as tradition has it, he was illiterate and unable to read the scriptures, his mind was so pure and penetrating that upon hearing one line from the Diamond Sutra he was enlightened. Often people would read scriptures to him so that he could explain to them the essential meaning.

He gave a very clear description of what the different schools, or vehicles, of Buddhism really mean.

> *Buddha preached the doctrine of three vehicles, and also that of the Supreme Vehicle. In trying to understand these, you should introspect your own mind and act independently of things and phenomena. The distinction of these four vehicles does not exist in the Dharma itself, but in the differentiation of people's minds. To see, to hear, and to recite the sutra is the Small Vehicle. To know the Dharma and to understand its meaning is the Middle Vehicle. To put the Dharma into actual practice is the Great Vehicle. To understand thoroughly all Dharmas, to have absorbed them completely, to be free from all attachments, and to be in possession of nothing, is the Supreme Vehicle.*

In all the traditions, whether it is the Indian, Burmese, Chinese, Japanese, Tibetan, or American, there are those who cling to the words, who recite the sutra. That is the Small Vehicle. As we put the words into practice, as we experience the Dharma, we progress through the vehicles until we are attached to nothing, in possession of nothing, living the Dharma fully, moment to moment. This is the Supreme Vehicle of the Dharma, the perfection of practice. It is not contained in any one tradition. It is contained in each person's evolution of understanding.

As different expressions of the Dharma unfolded historically great teachers used many skillful means in directing people to look into their own minds, to experience the Dharma within themselves. Some of the old familiar words, which had become a great bondage as concepts, were used in a new way to get people to see the reality of the moment.

Understanding the different usages of the word "Buddha," for example, greatly aids in understanding the various traditions which use the word in different ways. First, Buddha refers to the historical person, Siddhartha Gotama, who became fully enlightened. But it also means the mind free of defilement, Buddha-mind, Buddha-nature. The mind which is free of greed, hatred and delusion.

For 300 years after the Buddha's death there were no Buddha images. The people's practice was the image of the Buddha, there was no need to externalize it. But in time, as the practice was lost, people began to place the Buddha outside of their own minds, back in time and space. As the concept was externalized and images were made, great teachers started to reemphasize the other meaning of Buddha. There is a saying: "If you see the Buddha, kill him." Very shocking to people who offer incense and worship before an image. If you have a concept in the mind of a Buddha outside of yourself, kill it, let it go. There was an intense dialogue about realizing one's own Buddha-nature, becoming Buddha in a lifetime, seeing into one's Buddha-mind, and new life was breathed into the practice.

Gotama Buddha repeatedly reminded people that the experience of truth comes from one's own mind. There is the story of one monk so enraptured by the physical presence of the Buddha, who is said to have embodied physical as well as mental perfection, that he would sit very close to him at every opportunity and gaze at his physical form. After some time, the Buddha reprimanded him. He told the monk that he could gaze at this physical form for a hundred years and not see the Buddha. He who sees the Dharma sees the Buddha. The Buddha is within. It is the experience of the truth. Always bringing it back to the present moment, to the experience in the now.

Again from Hui Neng:

We should work for Buddhahood within the essence of mind. We should not look for it apart from ourselves. He who is kept in ignorance of his essence of mind is an ordinary being. He who is enlightened in his essence of mind is a Buddha.

Not Buddha as an historical person, but Buddha as freedom from defilements, purity of mind. That's the Buddha we all have to become.

Another concept which is often mistaken as differentiating traditions is the concept of bodhisattva. The word "bodhisattva" means two different things. In a very specific sense, it refers to a being who has vowed to attain supreme enlightenment, as did Siddhartha Gotama in his very long evolution to perfection. There is another meaning of bodhisattva, and that refers to all the forces of purity within the mind. In the Mahayana and Tibetan traditions, there is a whole pantheon of bodhisattvas, personifications of the forces within our minds. Manjusri is the bodhisattva of wisdom. Avalokiteshvara is the bodhisattva of compassion: manifestations of forces of purity within the mind. In every moment of wisdom we become Manjusri, in every moment of compassion we are Avalokiteshvara. If we understand bodhisattva in this way, the bodhisattva vows take on an expanded meaning.

In one sense, it is the vow taken in dedicating oneself to the supreme enlightenment of a Buddha. It is said of Siddhartha Gotama that many lifetimes ago, while in the presence of another Buddha, he had the capacity to become enlightened; but so inspired was he by that Buddha's presence, so moved by compassion for the suffering of all beings, he vowed to postpone his own enlightenment in order to bring to perfection all the qualities of Buddhahood. Although the freedom of mind in an enlightened being and in the Buddha is the same, the power and depth of a Buddha's wisdom and compassion is greater because of his immeasurably longer evolution.

154

Another meaning of the bodhisattva vow is described clearly by Hui Neng:

We vow to deliver an infinite number of sentient beings. Now what does that mean? It does not mean that I, Hui Neng, am going to deliver them. And who are these sentient beings within our minds? They are the delusive minds, the deceitful mind, the evil mind, and such like minds. All these are sentient beings. Each of them has to deliver himself by means of his own essence of mind.

The vow to deliver all sentient beings can be understood in the practice as delivering each being within us; to free the angry mind, the delusive mind, the greedy mind, the lustful mind. Each of these minds is a being, arising and passing away. And we vow to liberate all these beings, to free this process of mind from all defilement and impurity.

Another traditional difference in the various schools has to do with the idea of nirvana and samsara. One school talks about nirvana as something apart from the mind-body process; another talks of nirvana and samsara as being one. How to reconcile these two apparently contradictory statements? One way of understanding it is if you imagine a hurricane, a great wind revolving at a very high speed. At the center of these high velocity winds is a space of calm and stillness, the eye of the hurricane. From one perspective, the eye of the hurricane is very different from the winds. Everything is still, calm, very different from the whirlwind going on about it. From another perspective, one can see that both the wind and the eye are part of a unity, and can be described as a whole. In the same sense, from one perspective samsara and nirvana are very different. One is the continual process of change and the other is stillness and peace. From another perspective, they together constitute a unity and, in that sense, are one. In the *experience* of the Dharma, the words become clear. As long as we remain on the theoretical and conceptual level the words used by different schools seem to point to different truths. In fact, they are different fingers pointing to the same moon.

There is a powerful pointing to the truth in a description of the mind from a high Tibetan Tantric text. Try to experience the words rather than think about them:

There being really no duality, pluralism is untrue. Until duality is transcended and at-one-ment realized, enlightenment cannot be attained. The whole samsara and nirvana as an inseparable unity are one's mind. Owing to worldly beliefs which he is free to accept or reject, man wanders in samsara. Therefore, practicing the Dharma, freed from every attachment, grasp the whole essence of these teachings.

Although the One Mind is, it has no existence.

When one seeks one's mind in its true state, it is found to be quite intelligible, although invisible. In its true state, mind is naked, immaculate, not made of anything, being of the voidness, clear, vacuous, without duality, transparent, timeless, uncompounded, unimpeded, colorless, not realizable as a separate thing but as the unity of all things, yet not composed of them, of one taste, transcendent over differentiation.

The One Mind being verily of the voidness and without any foundation, one's mind is likewise as vacuous as the sky. To know whether this be so or not, look within thine own mind. Being merely a flux of instability like the air of the firmament, objective appearances are without power to fascinate and fetter. To know whether this be so or not, look within thine own mind. All appearances are verily one's own concepts, self-conceived in the mind, like reflections seen in a mirror. To know whether this be so or not, look within thine own mind. Arising of themselves and being naturally free like the clouds in the sky, all external appearances verily fade away into their own respective places. To know whether this be so or not, look within thine own mind.

The Dharma, being nowhere save in the mind, there is no other place for meditation but in the mind. The Dharma, being nowhere save in the mind, there is no other place of truth for the observance of a vow. The Dharma, being nowhere save in the mind, there is no Dharma elsewhere, whereby liberation can be attained.

One's mind is transparent, without quality. Being void of quality, it is comparable to a cloudless sky. It is the state of mind transcendent over all duality which brings liberation. Again and again, look within thine own mind.

When the Dharma is deeply understood it becomes clear that the essence of all practices leading to freedom is the same; that is, developing a mind which does not cling to anything at all. No preferences. No distinctions. No judgments. No clinging. No condemning. The practice is the same whether it is expressed through the words of the Sixth Patriarch in China or the Indian, Siddhartha Gotama.

Tilopa, a great Indian sage and the inspiration of one of the Tibetan lineages, taught this same balance of mind, here called Mahamudra, to his student Naropa.

Mahamudra is beyond all words and symbols, but for you Naropa, earnest and loyal, must this be said. The void needs no reliance. Mahamudra rests on nought. Without making an effort, but remaining loose and natural, one then breaks the yoke, thus gaining liberation. If with the mind, then one observes the mind, one destroys distinctions and reaches Buddhahood.

The clouds that wander through the sky have no roots, no home, nor do the distinctive thoughts floating through the mind. Once the self-mind is seen, discrimination stops.

In space, shapes and colors form, but neither by black nor white is space tinged. From the self-mind all things emerge. The mind by virtue and by vice is not stained.

. . . .

Do nought with the body but relax. Shut firm the mouth and silent remain. Empty your mind and think of nought. Like a hollow bamboo, rest at ease your body. Giving not, nor taking, put your mind at rest. Mahamudra is like a mind that clings to nought. Thus practicing, in time, you will reach Buddhahood.

. . . .

He who abandons craving and clings not to this or that perceives the real meaning given in the scriptures.

. . . .

At first a yogi feels his mind is tumbling like a waterfall; in mid-course like the Ganges, it flows on slow and gentle. In the end it is a great vast ocean where the lights of Son and Mother merge in One.

"He who abandons craving, and clings not to this or that, perceives the real meaning given in the scriptures." "Develop a mind which clings to nought." Abandon grasping, abandon attachment: the path to freedom.

The tradition of Dharma which evolved in Japan from the lineage of Hui Neng and other patriarchs produced a very beautiful literature and expression of the path, often very humorous. A story illustrating the same truths of non-attachment, and non-clinging, expressed in a very Zen-like way:

A university professor once visited a Japanese master, asking many questions about Zen. The master served tea, filling his guest's cup, and then continuing to pour. The professor watched the overflow exclaiming that the cup was full without room for any more. "Just like this cup," the master replied, "you are so full of your own views and opinions that there is no room for any new understanding. To experience the truth you must first empty your cup."

As long as there is an attachment to opinions and views, we can never experience the truth. "Do not seek the truth. Only cease to cherish opinions." In letting go of attachment to our own preconceptions, in that silence of mind, the whole Dharma is revealed. Each of us must empty our cup, empty our minds of attachment to views and beliefs.

There is such beauty and clarity in the different expressions of Dharma. We are fortunate in not having been brought up in a culture conditioned by any particular one, if we stay open enough to hear and appreciate them all. They are pointing to the same truth, to the experience of the Dharma within ourselves.

The Buddha advised, "Believe nothing merely because you have been told it, or because it is traditional, or because you yourself imagined it. Do not believe what your teacher tells you merely out of respect for the teacher. But whatever way, by thorough examination, you find to be one leading to good and happiness for all creatures, that path follow like the moon the path of the stars."

Question: *I'm confused about not having opinions. I mean, out in the world there are so many choices. . .*

Answer: Use the level of distinctions and preferences when appropriate, understanding that it is the conceptual level of mind, not the level of ultimate reality. Use the thought process without being attached to it. As explained in the Bhagavad-Gita, act without attachment to the fruit of the action. In the same way, our mind can be free of attachment to distinctions and preferences, yet using them when necessary for dealing with the world.

What about all the activities, like yoga, tai chi, pottery, weaving or whatever, as being part of spiritual practice?

Everything becomes possible when it is done with awareness, with clarity, without craving, without grasping, the whole world, the 10,000 joys and the 10,000 sorrows are all there to be experienced. The activity itself is no indication of depth or superficiality. The indication is the quality of mind in doing the activity. A tai chi master may be in perfect accordance with the Dharma. Perfect stillness of mind. Another person may be doing the same movements full of tension and striving. There are so many beautiful examples of all kinds of activities serving as an expression of perfection of mind. Many things become possible when the mind is free.

There is an idea that you first go through Hinayana and then Mahayana and then Vajrayana on the path, from one vehicle to the other with different kinds of things happening in each.

In the sense that you are referring to, Hinayana, Mahayana, and Vajrayana are stages on a path to realization. Whichever path one is following, these stages are going to be there. You can be following a Burmese tradition, or Japanese or Tibetan, and in any of them you will go through Hinayana, Mahayana, Vajrayana stages. Confusion arises because those terms also refer to different historical traditions. People confuse the stages on the path with the different historical and cultural expressions of the Dharma. For this reason, these concepts are perhaps not so useful. There are many stages along the path. They are to be experienced. The labeling of them is extraneous, and quite liable to be misunderstood. There is just what there is. There is the unfolding of the Dharma within oneself. We go through very many experiences. The experience, rather than the ideas and names about them, is what's most important.

There are different traditions of meditation in different countries. Would they too just be different ways of progressing on the path?

Mindfulness can be developed on any object. You can develop mindfulness on thoughts, on the body, on external objects, on internal objects, on all of them, or on some combination. The different techniques and methods are different ways of developing mindfulness. It is awareness which is the essence of all practices, that balance of mind out of which enlightenment happens. All things are impermanent, and insight can be developed on any object whatsoever. You can experience enlightenment in the middle of a thought, in the middle of a pain, while eating, while walking, any time at all, because it comes out of a perfect balance of mind, not by holding on to some particular object.

Some teachers talk about the danger of psychic powers in spiritual practice. What does that mean?

Power of mind can be developed. It is not wisdom. Power and wisdom are two very different things. It may be dangerous to develop those powers before reaching a high level of enlightenment, because they can just strengthen the idea of self, of ego, and be used in a very manipulative way. Power can be used skillfully if one has a firm foundation in morality and understanding, but it is not necessary to develop these powers. There are many enlightened beings without psychic powers, and there are many beings with powers who are not enlightened. In some people wisdom and power are combined.

In the Dhammapada, Buddha often refers to the state of attaining arahantship. Does that refer to the experience of enlightenment?

Yes, it refers to the complete elimination of greed, hatred, and delusion from the mind, which comes as the result of experiencing nirvana. The first experience of nirvana, the first glimpse of the ultimate truth, removes some of the defilements of mind; others remain. And as one continues to walk along the path, further defilements are uprooted. An arhant is one in whom all defilements are eradicated from the mind. In the same way, the idea of Buddhahood in this lifetime means freedom from greed, hatred and delusion. In the experience of the truth, the unity of the Dharma is understood. Develop a mind which clings to nought. This is the essence of all teachings. It becomes so simple when one practices.

What is needed to develop deep states of insight? Does it take something extraordinary?

There's only one thing that's required: to be aware of what's happening in the moment. If we have any idea at all of what should be happening, we're not fully experiencing the moment. The practice is to be mindful of all the changing states of mind and body without clinging, without condemning, without identifying with them. That's the path from beginning to end. Then it all unfolds by itself; there is nothing we have to do to make things happen. People don't believe how simple it is. There is often a desire to complicate it and to think that we have to experience some fantastic mental states. Rather, it's just sitting back very attentively and becoming the flow. Being simple and easy.

I thought that some paths stress service to others rather than freeing oneself first?

All paths revolve about seeing the illusory nature of self, of coming to the end of selfishness. The natural and organic expression of the Dharma is love and compassion, helping and caring for others. This has nothing to do with vehicle or path, or vow; it's the natural expression of wisdom. As we lose our attachment to the concept that this is "I" and that's "other," we begin to experience the unity of all beings, and from this understanding comes love and service.

As we get into practice, does this question of different paths disappear?

A poet-friend, Tom Savage, wrote a poem ending with these lines:

> Greater vehicle, lesser vehicle,
> No matter!
> All vehicles will be towed away
> at owner's expense.

•

Closing

You cannot stay on the summit forever. You have to come down again, so why bother in the first place? Just this. What is above knows what is below but what is below does not know what is above. One climbs and one sees; one descends and one sees no longer, but one has seen. There is an art of conducting oneself in the lower region by the memory of what one saw higher up. When one no longer sees, one can at least still know.

—Mount Analogue

The question now is how to integrate intensive meditation practice into one's everyday life. On one level, the answer is very simple: stay mindful. Even when there are distractions and a lot of input through the sense doors, if there is no clinging, no condemning, no expectations of how things should be, the mind will stay clear and balanced. Mindfulness is the greatest protection.

There are some things which will help maintain the balance and silence of mind. The most important of these is a daily sitting practice. Sitting twice every day for an hour at a time (or longer) will strengthen the concentration and mindfulness that has been cultivated during this month.

Having just finished an intensive retreat, sitting for one or two hours a day may seem quite easy, but as you resume your daily activities in the world, it will become more difficult to maintain. It will take discipline and effort. Give the sitting practice a high priority in the day, every day; arrange other activities around your meditation rather than trying to squeeze the sitting in between other things. You will begin to experience daily meditation as having a great transforming effect in your life.

It's helpful if you can arrange a set time to meditate each day, a time when you won't be disturbed. If you get in the habit of sitting at a particular time each day, there will be less likelihood of missing regular practice. A good time might be the first thing in the morning when you get up, as a way of setting up mindfulness for the day, and then an hour in the evening, which becomes a time of cooling out and relaxing the mind and body. Or, it could be any other time that's suitable for you. Experiment. The important thing is to maintain the continuity of your practice. A regular sitting practice is of inestimable value.

There are other things as well that you can do to integrate the practice into your life. Be mindful of certain activities which are done every day, such as eating. Try to eat one meal a day in silence. It will become a period of developing clear awareness, and will arouse all the tendencies in the mind which were cultivated this month. By repeating the exercise of mindfulness, you draw back the accumulated force of past practice.

In the course of daily activities we do a lot of walking. Make that a time of meditation. When walking you need not do the very slow "up, forward, down," except when appropriate; you can simply be aware of the whole body in movement, or of the touch of each step. Once again, experiment.

In moments of stress or tension during the day, remember the breath. With the eyes open, not making a show of meditation, be with either rising-falling or in-out, even for a few minutes. The mind will become concentrated and tranquil.

After some time you will find that mindfulness begins to follow you around in whatever you are doing. The Dharma is the totality of our lives. It does not mean only sitting or intensive meditation. The Dharma is everything, and we should live in harmony with that understanding.

The seeds of wisdom and compassion which have been planted and cultivated are powerful. They will bear fruit in varied and unexpected ways. At times when you feel most involved, most caught up in the world, there will be moments of strong awareness in which you will see yourself and the melodrama clearly. Be simple and easy. With a silent, peaceful mind, there is a natural unfolding of the Dharma.

There are some recollections which are helpful in our effort to live the Dharma from moment to moment. The first of these is remembering the truth of impermanence. Remember both your own impending death, and the changing nature of all phenomena in every moment. Stay aware of the flow, of the fact that everything is in ceaseless change, and the mind will be poised and balanced in all situations. You'll find yourself less judging of yourself, and less judging of others, making fewer rigid categorizations of people and situations. You will experience the possibility of living in a more open and empty way, responding spontaneously and creatively to each moment, without carrying around the burden of projections and preconceptions from the past.

The second recollection is that of love and compassion. When you relate to your parents, to your friends, to strangers, remember that on the deepest level there is no "I" and "other," no "we" and "them"; there is just a oneness, a unity of emptiness. Out of this emptiness emanates lovingkindness for all beings. Many painful elements of our relationships to other people fall away as we practice more love and compassion in our lives.

The Buddha gave an example of how this open gentleness of mind keeps us peaceful and balanced. If you put a spoonful of salt in a glass of water, the taste of all that water will be salty. But if you put the same amount of salt, or even a great deal more in a large pond, the taste will remain unaffected. In just the same way, when the mind is tight and rigid, any abrasive element has a stong and disturbing impact. When the mind is spacious and expansive, even more powerful negativities do not affect it. Lovingkindness is a soft and all embracing quality which we can make pervasive in our lives.

The third recollection is that of humility, or invisibility. There is no need to take your stance in the world as Mr. or Ms. Spiritual, as someone special. As Chuang Tzu wrote:

> *The man in whom Tao*
> *Acts without impediment*
> *Harms no other being*
> *By his actions*
> *Yet he does not know himself*
> *To be "kind," to be "gentle."*
>
> *The man in whom Tao*
> *Acts without impediment*
> *Does not bother with his own interests*
> *And does not despise*
> *Others who do.*
>
> *He does not struggle to make money*
> *And does not make a virtue of poverty.*
> *He goes his way*
> *Without relying on others*
> *And does not pride himself*
> *On walking alone.*
> *While he does not follow the crowd*
> *He won't complain of those who do.*
> *Rank and reward*
> *Make no appeal to him;*

Disgrace and shame
Do not deter him.
He is not always looking
For right and wrong
Always deciding "Yes" or "No."
The ancients said, therefore:
"The man of Tao
Remains unknown
Perfect virtue
Produces nothing
'No-Self'
Is 'True-Self.'
And the greatest man
Is Nobody."

You will discover that the more invisible you are, the more simple and easy your life becomes. Again from Chuang Tzu:

If a man is crossing a river
And an empty boat collides with his own skiff,
Even though he be a bad-tempered man
He will not become very angry.
But if he sees a man in the boat,
He will shout at him to steer clear.
If the shout is not heard, he will shout again,
And yet again, and begin cursing.
And all because there is somebody in the boat.
Yet if the boat were empty,
He would not be shouting, and not angry.

If you can empty your own boat
Crossing the river of the world,
No one will oppose you,
No one will seek to harm you.

167

Empty your boat, go through life in an open and empty and loving way, and "no one will oppose you, no one will seek to harm you."

Many of you have asked how to tell other people about the Dharma. One of the most important qualities to develop in sharing on all levels is to learn very skillfully how to listen, to be sensitive to the situation and to the other person. In that silence of mind, when we are really paying attention, the proper mode of communication becomes apparent. Do not hold on to any particular conceptual expression of the Dharma, or any preconceived way of being. Don't hold on to anything. Sometimes what is called for is a very ordinary conversation, relating in a simple and easy way. There is a great skill involved in learning how to listen. Be open and accepting of others. Receptivity and emptiness of self makes possible a wide range of understanding and sharing.

The literal meaning of Vipassana is to see things clearly, not only our own mind-body process, although that is basic, but to see everything clearly, other people, relationships, situations. The Way is to live without greed, without hatred, without delusion; to live with awareness, with wakefulness, and equanimity, and with love. We are the truth unfolding, and a one month retreat, or a lifetime of practice, are just beginnings in the awesome task of true understanding.

> *Great knowledge is all encompassing; small knowledge is limited.*
> *Great words are inspiring; small words are chatter. . . When we are*
> *awake, our senses open. We get involved with our activities and our*
> *minds are distracted. Sometimes we are hesitant, sometimes under-*
> *handed, and sometimes secretive. Little fears cause anxiety, and great*
> *fears cause panic. Our words fly off like arrows, as though we knew*
> *what was right and wrong. We cling to our own point of view, as*
> *though everything depended on it. And yet our opinions have no*
> *permanence: like autumn and winter, they gradually pass away. We*

are caught in the current and cannot return. We are tied up in knots like an old clogged drain; we are getting closer to death with no way to regain our youth. Joy and anger, sorrow and happiness, hope and fear, indecision and strength, humility and willfulness, enthusiasm and insolence, like music sounding from an empty reed, or mushrooms rising from the warm dark earth, continually appear before us day and night. No one knows whence they come. Don't worry about it! Let them be! How can we understand it all in one day?

For further information and schedules
of Vipassana meditation retreats
you may contact the

Insight Meditation Society
Barre, Mass. 01005

SUGGESTED READING LIST

Being Nobody, Going Nowhere, Ayya Khema
Being Peace, Thich Nhat Hanh
Chariot to Nibbana, Sayadaw U Pandita
The Heart of Buddhist Meditation, Nyaniponika Thera
The Meditative Mind, Daniel Goleman
Miracle of Mindfulness, Thich Nhat Hanh
*Practical Insight Meditation, Mahasi Sayadaw
†Seeking the Heart of Wisdom, Joseph Goldstein & Jack
   Kornfield
A Still Forest Pool, edited by Jack Kornfield & Paul Brieter
The Sutta-Nipata, translated by H. Saddhatissa
Thus Have I Heard, translated by Maurice Walshe
The Vision of Dhamma, Nyaniponika Thera
What the Buddha Taught, Walpola Rahula
Zen Mind, Beginner's Mind, Shunryu Suzuki

Cassette recordings of Joseph Goldstein's talks can be
obtained from:

> Dharma Seed
> Insight Meditation Society
> Pleasant Street
> Barre, Massachusetts 01005

---

*Available from the Buddhist Publication Society, Box 61, Kandy, Sri Lanka
†Published by Shambhala Publications, Inc. *The Path of Insight Meditation,* an audio tape
of *Seeking the Heart of Wisdom,* read by Joseph Goldstein, is available from Shambhala
Lion Editions.

SHAMBHALA DRAGON EDITIONS

Living with Kundalini: The Autobiography of Gopi Krishna.

The Lotus-Born: The Life Story of Padmasambhava, by Yeshe Tsogyal. Translated by Erik Pema Kunsang.

Mastering the Art of War, by Zhuge Liang & Liu Ji. Translated & edited by Thomas Cleary.

The Mysticism of Sound and Music, by Hazrat Inayat Khan.

The Myth of Freedom and the Way of Meditation, by Chögyam Trungpa.

Rational Zen: The Mind of Dogen Zenji, translated by Thomas Cleary.

Returning to Silence: Zen Practice in Daily Life, by Dainin Katagiri. Foreword by Robert Thurman.

Seeking the Heart of Wisdom: The Path of Insight Meditation, by Joseph Goldstein & Jack Kornfield. Foreword by H. H. the Dalai Lama.

Shambhala: The Sacred Path of the Warrior, by Chögyam Trungpa.

The Shambhala Dictionary of Buddhism and Zen.

The Spiritual Teaching of Ramana Maharshi, by Ramana Maharshi. Foreword by C. G. Jung.

Tao Teh Ching, by Lao Tzu. Translated by John C. H. Wu.

Teachings of the Buddha, revised & expanded edition. Edited by Jack Kornfield.

The Tibetan Book of the Dead: The Great Liberation through Hearing in the Bardo. Translated with commentary by Francesca Fremantle & Chögyam Trungpa.

Vitality, Energy, Spirit: A Taoist Sourcebook. Translated & edited by Thomas Cleary.

The Way of the Bodhisattva, by Shantideva. Translated by the Padmakara Translation Group.

Wen-tzu: Understanding the Mysteries, by Lao-tzu. Translated by Thomas Cleary.

Zen Essence: The Science of Freedom. Translated & edited by Thomas Cleary.